**The Pathways Of Prayer**

# COMMUNION WITH GOD

The Pathways Of Prayer

# COMMUNION WITH GOD

**Sister Immaculata, O.C.D.**
**A Carmelite Nun**

**Our Sunday Visitor, Inc.**
**Huntington, Indiana 46750**

*Nihil Obstat:*
  David A. Dillon, S.T.D.
  *Censor Librorum/Deputatus*

*Imprimatur:*
  ✠John R. Roach, D.D.
  Archbishop of St. Paul and Minneapolis
  May 17, 1978

ISBN: 0-87973-639-9
Library of Congress Catalog Card Number: 78-60487

Cover Design by Becky O'Brien

Published, printed and bound in the U.S.A. by
Our Sunday Visitor, Inc.
Noll Plaza
Huntington, Indiana 46750

639

# Contents

## PART 1: PRAYER

I     Esteem for Prayer / 4

II    Prayer and Divine Providence / 6

III   Prayer Depends on God's Self-Revelation to Us and Our Response in Faith / 23

IV   Recollection and the Practice of the Presence of God / 28

     A.   The Presence of God Is the Key to the Spiritual Life and to Purity of Conscience / 29

     B.   How Do We Attain to This Holy Recollection in God's Presence? / 37

         • Purity of Conscience / 37

         • Fidelity to this Practice in Faith /

         • To Perform All Our Actions in His Presence / 39

V     Forms of Prayer / 46

     A.   Vocal Prayer / 46

     B.   Mental Prayer / 51

         • Meditation — The First Water / 53

         • The Carmelite Method of Meditation / 70

     C.   The Prayer of Recollection or Simplicity / 86

# PART 2: THE CALL TO CONTEMPLATION

VI     The Call / 97

VII    How Do We Prepare Ourselves for the Life of Prayer? / 102

      A. To Realize the Great Dignity and Capacity of Our Souls and Take Care of Them / 102

      B. To Strive for Perfect Conformity with the Will of God / 103

         • Courage and Resolution in Bearing Trials / 104

         • Helpful Means of Perseverance / 114

          Cultivation of Joy / 114

          Faith / 115

          Patience and Persistence / 116

          Not to Be Afflicted / 116

          Prudent Balance in Life / 118

          Never Give Up Prayer / 119

      C. Mortification Specifically Adapted to Prayer / 120

      D. Prudence in Attending to Ourselves and to God / 122

VIII   Prayer: Friendship with God / 124
       A. God's Ways of Dealing with the Soul in
          Prayer / 125
       B. Our Dispositions Toward Him:
          Littleness / 127
IX     The Apostolate of Prayer / 130
       A. Prayer Is Service / 130
       B. The Power of This Service / 132
X      Our Mother Mary and Her Place in Our
       Communion with God / 133
XI     Conclusion / 138
XII    Personal Notes and Comments / 144

# Acknowledgments

The author and publisher wish to thank all those who made this book possible, and are especially grateful to the following for permission to use their copyrighted material:

*The Documents of Vatican II*, General Editor Walter M. Abbott, S.J., Translation Editor V. Rev. Monsignor Joseph Gallagher. Reprinted with permission of *America*. All rights reserved. ©1978 by America Press, Inc., 106 West 56th St., New York, N.Y. 10019.

*The Collected Works of St. John of the Cross*, translated by Kieran Kavanaugh and Otilio Rodriguez, ©1965 by Washington Province of Discalced Carmelites, Inc. Paperback edition published by ICS Publications, 2131 Lincoln Road, N.E., Washington, D.C.

*Story of a Soul*, by John Clarke, O.C.D., ©1975/1976 by Washington Province of Discalced Carmelites, Inc. ICS Publications, 2131 Lincoln Road, N.E., Washington, D.C.

*The Practice of the Presence of God*, Lawrence of the Resurrection, O.C.D., ©1952, Newman Press. Reprinted with permission of Paulist Press, 545 Island Rd., Ramsey, N.J. 07446.

*Spiritual Legacy*, Mary of the Trinity, P.C., edited by Van den Broek, O.F.M. ©1950, Newman Press. Reprinted with permission of Paulist Press.

*Way of Divine Love*, Sister Josepha Menendez, R.S.C.J. ©1950, Newman Press. Reprinted with permission of Paulist Press.

*Dialogues*, Catherine of Siena, ©1943, Newman Press. Reprinted with permission of Paulist Press.

*Life and Revelations of St. Gertrude*, translation by

Part 1

# PRAYER

We are called to commune with God; we do not just decide to do it on our own initiative. This call to enter into a personal union with God is the specific purpose of our creation: that we may know Him, love Him, serve Him and be happy with Him forever. The Second Vatican Council has stressed four principal themes which are repeated throughout most of the Documents; they are: (I) the *vocation of man*[1] which is a call addressed to his (II) *conscience*[2] urging him to a (III) *conversion* of life[3] in these particularly crucial times, and this call is precisely to (IV) *commune with Him*.

> An outstanding cause of human dignity lies in man's call to communion with God. From the very circumstances of his origin, man is already invited to converse with God. For man would not exist were he not created by God's love and constantly preserved by it. And he cannot fully live according to truth unless he freely acknowledges that love and devotes himself to his Creator. ("The Church in the Modern World," 19, *The Documents of Vatican II*, Walter M. Abbot, S.J., and Joseph Gallagher, editors, N.Y., America Press, 1966, p.215)

It is a marvelous privilege to lift up our souls to God in prayer, that we should have Him within us and that He should allow us to come into His presence at any time and ask for whatever we want and need. We can say that the whole of religion rests

---

[1] Dogmatic Constitution on the Church, Par. 3
[2] The Church in the Modern World, Par. 16
[3] Declaration on Religious Freedom, Par. 3

on prayer, and the life of the conscience — the moral life — rests on prayer. A lengthy quote from St. Gregory of Nyssa on the Lord's Prayer (Sermon 1) says this so well and is so pertinent, it might have been written for our own times:

> If work is preceded by prayer, sin will find no entrance into the soul. For when the consciousness of God is firmly established in the heart, the devices of the devil remain sterile, and matters of dispute will always be settled according to justice. Prayer prevents the farmer from committing sin, for his fruit will multiply even on a small plot of land, so that sins no longer enter together with desire for more. It is the same with everyone, with the traveller, with somebody who prepares an expedition or a marriage. Whatever anyone may set out to do, if it is done with prayer the undertaking will prosper and he will be kept from sin, because there is nothing to oppose him and drag the soul into passion. If, on the other hand, a man leaves God out and gives his attention to nothing but his business, then he is inevitably opposed to God, because he is separated from Him. For a person who does not unite himself to God through prayer is separated from God. . . .
>
> Therefore we must learn first of all that we ought always to pray and not to faint. For the effect of prayer is union with God, and if someone is with God, he is separated from the enemy. Through prayer we guard our chastity, control our temper, and rid ourselves of vanity; it makes us forget injuries, overcomes envy, defeats injustice, and makes amends for a sin. Through prayer we obtain physical well-being, a happy home, and a strong, well-ordered society. Prayer

will make our nation powerful, will give us victory in war and security in peace; it reconciles enemies and preserves allies. Prayer is the seal of virginity and a pledge of faithfulness in marriage; it shields the wayfarer, protects the sleeper, and gives courage to those who keep vigil. It obtains a good harvest for the farmer and a safe port for the sailor.

Prayer is your advocate in lawsuits. If you are in prison, it will obtain your release; it will refresh you when you are weary and comfort you when you are sorrowful. Prayer is the delight of the joyful as well as solace to the afflicted. It is the wedding crown of the spouses and the festive joy of a birthday no less than the shroud that enwraps us in death.

Prayer is intimacy with God and contemplation of the invisible. It satisfies our yearnings and makes us equal to the angels. Through it good prospers, evil is destroyed, and sinners will be converted. Prayer is the enjoyment of things present and the substance of the things to come. Prayer turned the whale into a home for Jonas; it brought Ezechias back to life from the very gates of death; it transformed the flames into a moist wind for the Three Children. Through prayer the Israelites triumphed over the Amalecites, and 185,000 Assyrians were slain in one night by the invisible sword. Past history furnishes thousands of other examples beside these which make it clear that of all the things valued in this life nothing is more precious than prayer. (*Ancient Christian Writers*, No. 18, pp. 23-25)

# I. ESTEEM FOR PRAYER

If we as Christians have been called to live a life of prayer, we must begin with a surpassing esteem for prayer. This is a very obvious statement but one which cannot be too deeply impressed on our minds. Perhaps in theory our wills acknowledge the supremacy of prayer but in practice other things come first under pretext of need or service. There is no such thing as living a Christian life if we are still a little hesitant about the efficacy of prayer.

> Do we believe in the power of prayer? When temptation threatens to make us fall, when light does not shine in us, when the cross is hard to carry, do we have recourse to prayer, as Christ advised us to? Do we not doubt its efficacy, if not in principle at least in practice? Yet we know Christ's promise: "Ask and it shall be given to you." We know the common teaching of theologians: that true prayer, by which we ask for ourselves with humility, confidence, and perseverance the graces necessary for our salvation, is infallibly efficacious. We know this doctrine, and yet it seems to us at times that we have truly prayed without being heard.
>
> We believe in, or rather we see, the power of a machine, of an army, of money, and of knowledge; but we do not believe strongly enough in the efficacy of prayer. *(The Three Ages of the Interior Life*, Garrigou-Lagrange Vol. I, p. 429)

God the Almighty and Infinite Being, the Creator and Governor of the universe is the Rock on which our prayer rests, and the entire worth of any prayer depends on the degree of living faith a person has in God's willingness to give what we ask.

By the very remembrance of all the benefits we have already received from God we should lift up our hearts and sustain our courage to persevere in prayer. Even a very little personal experience of the Lord's bounty in answering prayer multiplies our esteem for prayer and our confidence in asking.

We can see from Scripture how much God promised in the prophecies of the Messiah to come. He was to be a redeemer and savior, a king and merciful lawgiver, yet who would have been so bold as to say this Messiah would be God Himself!

God promises much but He gives much more! He foretold a savior and behold, we received a God-man Redeemer, a Father and a Bridegroom Who died personally for each of us through terrible suffering and rose again in order that we too might live an entirely new spiritual existence, expecting even the resurrection of our own bodies. Who would have dared to ask for so much! Who would have dared to believe so much out of the hidden prophecies of the Old Testament! Even now after it has all been so gloriously accomplished, many do not yet believe it.

If He redeemed us at such a personal cost, surely He will hear our prayers when we ask for the gifts He suffered such torments to give us. A very great part of His anguish, so to speak, is that we do not ask enough. We do not believe enough in His ardent desire to give Himself, to reveal Himself, to fill us with Himself. We have only to make the initial sign that we want to pray to Him, and He is already there, eager to grant whatever we ask. It is His joy to answer prayer, not only that of the saints, but even the most humble request of the least among men. If only we understood that, our lives would be transformed and we would cease to plod along in boring mediocrity. Our hours of prayer would be filled with all the thrill of a breathtaking adventure.

> Merit, being a right to a reward, is related to divine justice; prayer, on the other hand, is addressed to divine mercy, which often hears and grants it and lifts up the soul without any merit on its part, thus it raises up souls that have fallen into the state of spiritual death. The most wretched man, from the depths of the abyss into which he has fallen, can utter this cry to mercy, which is prayer. The beggar who possesses nothing but his poverty can pray in the very name of his wretchedness, and, if he puts his whole heart into his petition, mercy inclines toward him, the abyss of wretchedness calls to that of mercy. The soul is raised up, and God is glorified. We should recall the conversion of Magdalen. (Lagrange, op. cit. p. 428)

## II. PRAYER AND DIVINE PROVIDENCE

All prayer is founded on the mystery of Divine Providence. Divine Providence is the master plan of the government of creation. Through and by means of Divine Providence the planets revolve and the smallest details of life are arranged, even the ones we tend to overlook or to consider as mere chance. It is the work of recollection through faith to train us to see the action of God in even the most seemingly inconsequential events.

God's Providence is His Master mind planning all the good His love wishes to accomplish, and when we speak of His Providence we understand His Divine will irresistibly carrying out His master plans. We know God is all good and merciful, and that He desires the happiness of all His creation. Therefore, Divine Providence is the Creator's continual creation of life and goodness and His continual and infinite determination to do good, to diffuse good and to overcome all forces against that good. Divine Providence is God's unconquerable will to save His creation directed by His unmatchable genius in doing so. God loves, therefore He loves to create masterpieces of His love: human spirits who can love in return. He loves to show His Divine power to love in their behalf by ordering all the great and small happenings of their lives.

But Providence is a mystery to us simply because the Divine intelligence exceeds our human intelligence. Even if God told us His plans we would not understand . . . and part of His plan is that we win our salvation through faith, by which we see, yet in darkness. Faith is a superhuman power given to the intellect by which the human mind can gain knowledge and understanding (light) above and beyond its natural capacity of knowing and reasoning. St. Thomas tells us that faith is an adequate means of knowledge. Through it we can come to know that which would otherwise be impossible for the human mind to know; that is, the Divine mysteries of God, the plans of the Divine mind and the knowledge of the will of God, the Law of God.

God's Providence has two aspects, two parts, so

to speak: a part of His will or plan made known to us, and a part hidden from us. Faith is necessary for both. God's will is made known to us through revelation contained in Sacred Scripture. Without faith we cannot understand it because we do not believe it. We must believe in order to know what the Son of God revealed to us of the Father's will. Through the teachings of the Gospel and the guiding directives of the Church, the Christian's daily duty is defined. We enter into God's Providence in His known will by our fidelity to our duty. But there is another aspect of the Divine Providence above our capacity and that is more properly the mystery of His Providence: His unknown will. This too is the object of supernatural faith, sometimes more so, but not always. It takes an enormous faith to live the known will of God in a secular society, sometimes more than to accept a sudden accident or upset or even a death.

When we speak of the unknown will of God, it does not mean that the events involved or our response is unknown to us; it means that we do not understand the reasons behind it or we are not able to see the good that will come out of it. But known or unknown, the will of God requires constant and tremendous faith.

Let us also remember that faith is a principle of knowledge. Faith is a supernatural light given to the mind of man by which it may see into divine truths. When we speak of accepting the will of God in faith, it does not mean that we are always totally in the dark. The man who believes sees; and the more he believes the more he sees. We have often heard that we must accept the will of God blindly. There is a truth in that statement. We must accept what we do not understand, what we cannot avoid; but when we believe in the Love that governs our lives, when we believe that "all things work together unto the good of those who love Him" (Romans 8:28), then we are not left without light, because faith sees. Faith gradually begins to penetrate why this or that painful event happened.

When we believe in love, the Divine Love that surrounds us and wills to lead us home, we can never think of the Providence of God as a blinding force to which we must submit our minds without thinking, as though we were being swept along with the current of a river out into an even greater ocean of the unknown. When we believe, we know that we are being guided somewhere; we may not know where, but we do know Whose is the love that is guiding us. With every duty responded to and with every difficulty or trial accepted, our faith grows stronger and so more clearly penetrates the Divine Love behind every action, behind every detail whether sweet or bitter.

The present moment is ever filled with infinite treasures; it contains more than you have capacity to hold. Faith is the measure. Believe, and it will be done to you accordingly. Love also is the measure. The more the heart loves, the more it desires; and the more it desires, so much the more will it receive. The will of God presents itself to us at each moment as an immense ocean that no human heart can fathom; but what the heart can receive from this ocean is equal to the measure of our faith, confidence and love. The whole of creation cannot fill the human heart,

9

for the heart's capacity surpasses all that is not God. The mountains that are terrifying to look at, are but atoms for the heart. The Divine will is an abyss of which the present moment is the entrance. Plunge into this abyss and you will always find it infinitely more vast than your desires. Do not flatter anyone, nor worship your own illusions; they can neither give you anything nor take anything from you. You will receive your fulness from the will of God alone, which will not leave you empty. Adore it, put it first, before all other things.

When the will of God is made known to a soul, and has made the soul realize His willingness to give Himself to it — provided that the soul, too, gives itself to God — then under all circumstances the soul experiences a great happiness in this coming of God, and enjoys it the more, the more it has learned to abandon itself at every moment to His most adorable will. *(Abandonment to Divine Providence*, Caussade, Book I, ch. 2)

"Accepting the will of God" has sometimes become synonomous with passively enduring some evil we cannot avoid. It is not always so. The mysterious events of Providence also contain unexpected joys: a tribute, a triumph, a promotion, a surprise visit from an old friend, the consolation of a loved one, a spiritual grace given suddenly and gratuitously because our Father saw that we needed it now. As we must surrender and accept the hard things, we must be grateful for both, because both are equally grace, the grace of the will of God. When good things come, we must acknowledge them from God and not just treat them as chance happenings . . . and when the bad things befall us, we must also accept with humble trust and gratitude, blessing the action of God in joy and in pain.

Abandonment to Divine Providence does not mean that we do nothing. God is a Father and a Lover. No father wants a listless child; no lover could delight in an unresponsive bride. God likes cooperation from the heart. We have to put forth an effort to know His will, to understand where our duty lies. We do that by studying the Gospel and learning the teachings of the Church. But also in the matter of those events which we cannot avoid, accepting is a positive act. It means that we act along with His will; that we ratify the Divine will; that we say "yes" to it, even when we do not understand.

Abandonment is love in action. But even our love stems from the will of God; it is part of His Providence. He wills that His love should flow through all His creation freely, that is, by the free choice of His children willing to love in return and to repay such love with love. There is no purer love than to make the Divine will our own and to totally give ourselves to His good pleasure, accepting tranquilly whatever He does in our lives.

St. John of the Cross speaks strongly of the importance of abandoning ourselves to God in order to preserve our peace of soul. In the following passage he tells us that the whole mind, especially the memory, must be surrendered to God in faith and hope.

> The afflictions and disturbances engendered in a soul through adversities are no help in remedying these adversities; rather, distress and

worry ordinarily makes things worse and even does harm to the soul itself. Thus David proclaims: Indeed every man is disturbed in vain. (Psalms 38:7). Clearly, it is always vain to be disturbed, since being disturbed is never any help.

Thus if the whole world were to crumble and come to an end and all things were to go wrong, it would be useless to get disturbed, for this would do more harm than good. The endurance of all with tranquil and peaceful equanimity not only reaps many blessings, but also helps the soul so that in these very adversities it may succeed in judging them and employing the proper remedy.

Solomon, having clear knowledge of this harm and this advantage, exclaimed: I knew there was nothing better for man than to rejoice and do good in his life. (Ecclesiastes 3:12). By this he indicates that in all events, however unfavorable, we ought to rejoice rather than be disturbed, and bear them all with equanimity so as not to lose a blessing greater than all prosperity: tranquillity of soul and peace in all things, in adversity as well as in prosperity. *(Ascent of Mount Carmel*, Book III, ch. 6:3-4, Kavanaugh trs. p. 223)

Abandonment to the will of God simplifies our whole lives and the interior of our souls. It does not mean leaving aside human effort, common sense, normal foresight or careful planning. It means we give ourselves freely to His Word. It is the surrender to the impression of the Divine Word in our lives as Jesus surrendered to it. Even though He always was the Divine Word from eternity, He became the Word in the flesh of human nature in order to show us how to carry out the word in a world that is always putting up obstacles against it. We can do nothing greater than to give ourselves completely to Him so that He can live again in us to carry out His own will.

Peaceful abandonment; there is no greater gift to God. It is the crowning of our lives and the highest tribute to the Divine Majesty. It is the greatest worship, the worship Jesus asked for "in spirit and truth." It makes our whole life an act of worship and adoration no matter what we do. It is what the Lord asked when He said: "Abide in My love" . . . remain in it, and you will have done everything to please Me. It is the one thing necessary.

Yes, it simplifies our lives and greatly relieves the burden of life. Once we have done our duty we can rely on God to do the rest. Even without their seeing the results, God keeps leading abandoned souls, those who are His children, upward toward their goal of sanctity, which is union with His will. Supported by His known will in our duties, and surrendered to the hidden will of God, in fidelity coupled with abandonment, we give Him our whole life, past, present and future. We are freed from a thousand perplexities as to what we should do. We are freed from the terrible inner weight of nameless anxieties over our responsibilities, from fears or past guilt. If we are in the will of God we have nothing to fear. Nothing can harm us either from hell or from earth, because we are protected by the power of God. If we are doing His will, nothing else is required of us.

Abandonment simplifies the inner man also.

The disorder in our souls is there as the result of sin. Sin is the exercising of our own will contrary to the will of God. Sin disorients us from God, ourselves, and from others. It is the essence of disorder, disunity and inner torment. A disordered soul is torn from within. Doubts, fears, perplexities and confusions invade it and when it turns to prayer it is full of distracting, even tormenting thoughts. But once we have brought our wills into oneness with the will of God, the order is gradually restored. We learn to fear nothing because we experience the security we have in Him. Doubt begins to fade away as we exercise our faith, as we positively will to believe in His care for us. Perplexity and confusion are dispelled as the light of the understanding of God's manner of acting with the souls He loves comes to be a personal experience. Distractions lessen and we find that they do not draw us away from God in prayer because we have learned what it "feels" like to be rooted in His will in faith so that we understand what St. Paul meant when he said: "Who can separate us from the love of Christ?" (Romans 8:35)

Who can separate us from the will of God if we have come to appreciate our treasure? Who can take His will from us when it is our will too? "In His will is our peace," says Dante, following St. Augustine; yes, our peace, our security, our life and vitality, our inner unity and our eternal happiness.

The measure of our abandonment is the measure of our sanctity. Those who are most intimately united to God cannot pray for anything intensely or desire anything ardently except on condition that it be the holy will of God in which is all their life. They live in it as fish in water.

Whatever their minds conceive or their hearts desire to pray for is always prefaced by: If it be Your will, Lord, because they know that nothing good is done outside of His will.

The difference between a good person and a saint is a simple but continuous "yes" to Divine Love.

All our merit consists not in what we have done but in the part of our lives that we have surrendered to Christ to live in us. This abandonment of ourselves to Him so that His life is all we have through the will of God, is the heart of sanctity. Abandonment makes us the little children of the Gospel more than anything else. It is both the way up the mountain and the summit. All our prayer must aim at this: to remove the obstacles so that we allow God to act in us, through Christ living in us.

St. Therese of Lisieux, the little Queen of Abandonment, expresses this perfectly when she says that toward the end of her life she had no other means of going to God than simple abandonment to love. This is the perfection of Faith:

Now I have no further desire unless it be to love Jesus even unto folly! Love alone draws me. I wish for neither suffering nor death, yet both are precious to me, and I have long called upon them as the messengers of joy. Already I have suffered much; already it has seemed to me that my barque was nearing the Eternal Shore. From my earliest years I believed the Little Flower would be gathered in her springtime, but now the spirit of self-abandonment is my sole guide — I have no other compass. I am no longer able to ask eagerly for anything save the perfect accomplishment of God's designs on my soul. (*Autobiography of St. Therese*, ch. 8)

It is prayer that leads us to such an appreciation of Divine Providence that the soul can reach this state of abandonment to it. Prayer opens the gates of the treasures of the Divine will. It is founded on Divine Providence because our only reason for living is to do the will of God. We pray, not just for what we want but in order, above all, to be able to accomplish the will of God.

The Liturgy of the Church, the official prayer of Christ on earth, is full of meditations on the wisdom of God's will and His Providence in leading His people. It speaks often of the happiness of the just man who always seeks to know and do the will of God, and it almost always ends with a petition that we be able to accomplish His will; that no evil force may prevent us from living in His will.

They are happy whose life is blameless, who follow God's law. They are happy who do His will, seeking Him with all their hearts, who never do anything evil but walk in His ways. You have laid down your precepts to be obeyed with care. May my footsteps be firm to obey your statutes. Then I shall not be put to shame as I heed your commands. (Psalms 119:1-6)

Lord, make me know your ways. Lord, teach me your paths. Make me walk in your truth, and teach me; for you are God my savior. The Lord is good and upright. He shows the path to those who stray. He guides the humble in the right path; he teaches his way to the poor. (Psalms 25)

If anyone fears the Lord, he will show him the path he should choose. His soul shall live in happiness. . . . (Psalms 25)

Keep me from the way of error and teach me your law. (Psalms 119)

Remember your word to your servant by which you gave me hope. This is my comfort in sorrow, that your promise gives me life. (Psalms 119:49)

As we pray we begin to see into the transcendent darkness of Divine things. God illumines the soul that prays. When the hand of God seems to deal out only adversities, bitterness and afflictions, we are made to turn to Him for help in our trials. We are almost forced to pray, and in prayer we learn the great lesson of Scripture:

Before I was afflicted, I strayed, but now I keep your word. It was good for me to be afflicted, to learn your will.

Lord, I know that your decrees are right, that you have afflicted me justly. (Psalms 119:57)

We learn God and His ways; we learn humility in dealing with Him; we learn to revere His majesty because we see that in our prosperity we were walking in darkness, and if not in serious sin, at least we were living for ourselves, with that dullness to Divine realities which can never be cleared away without the cleansing power of suffering. It is through prayer that we penetrate into the secret and hidden mysteries of the Divine will. We see and experience that we only knew abstractly before, namely, that God's infinite ways are so much above us that we must suffer before we can see.

We learn that there is grace for every trial; that God really *is* with us in suffering. He never presses down without holding us up with the other hand. No, we may not see where we are going but need we see when we are being led? The light that is given may not be exactly the light that we want, the light that will answer our demands to understand why He is being so hard on us. The light that we are given shows us that we are sinners and we dare not demand to know. We are illumined by a light that will feed us with the sweet peace of humility. We understand that we can trust His desire to do good for us; that what He takes away He only seems to take away in order to give us something greater. We learn that what He does not grant in one way He will grant in another. If He closes a door it is to keep us from going through it to our own loss. If He shuts up our path with "square stones" (Lamentations 3:9) it is to keep us from going astray. If He hinders and brings to nothing all our plans and aspirations, it is to show us how much we were working for our own profit. If He lets our lives turn to failure, it is to keep us from sin.

We come to understand that He wants us to love Him and cling to Him in situations we cannot understand. Peaceful abandonment is always profitable to us. Through it we see that it is His merciful love that is pursuing us through trials and adversities. He wants to bring the proud heart to surrender; He wants to soothe the fearful heart with trust — because the proud one does not want to surrender to a power above himself or to admit his need to depend on God's loving providence . . . and the fearful one mistrusts his own ability to remain in grace because he has not yet learned by experience that it is God Who keeps him in grace.

It is by prayer that we enter into the Divine Plan. Prayer itself is a part of the Divine Government. In His almighty power and wisdom God ordained from the beginning that the men He would create would be like Himself with spiritual powers of intelligence and will. Then He made them His children by grace, desiring that they become capable of assisting Him in governing all creation. He gave Adam mastery over Paradise and thus over the whole world of created nature . . . so that Adam would be like his Father. God wanted His sons and daughters to take their place in mature government, and become in turn lords of the world.

We govern with God the more we become like Him. We become like Him by doing His will to the extent that it is our will. When His will and ours is one we take on the power of God Himself. The work of making the Divine will ours is the work of faith and prayer. The first devotion of all devotions is to the will of God. The first reason for praying is for the grace to do the will of God. We meditate on the works of God in creation and in history in order to see what God has done, and our reflections fill us with images of what He must be like. We meditate on Scripture, especially the Gospel, to understand His work in the redemption and what He requires of us in order to partake of that redemption. We praise Him for His works and for His grace; we adore Him and bless Him in prayer and we then petition Him for what we need . . . but all our needs can be summed up in one which is the grace of all graces:

the grace to do His will, for by that we are doing everything. Scripture teaches us the primacy of the will of God and in the Psalms it asks a blessing of God to be able to do His will.

> Bless your servant and I shall live and obey your word. Open my eyes that I may see the wonders of your law. I am a pilgrim on the earth; show me your commands. My soul is ever consumed as I long for your decrees. (Psalms 119)

We enter His Providence by prayer; we accept His will, sweet or painful, by prayer. We conform our wills to His by prayer and we learn to know His Mind in prayer. Prayer is the link between our finite spirits and God's infinite Spirit. Prayer is the window through which the Divine Light of God's Mind floods into the darkness of our finite minds. In prayer we learn that if we do not get our wills we will get His will which always works better. We may face disappointment in what we planned but if we accept that as His will, we will earn the most precious of all graces: the friendship of God.

Our prayer will not change His immutable will, but we know that in His wisdom He foresaw our future prayers and included them in the mystery of His dispositions of Providence. We pray not that we may change the Divine dispositions but that we may obtain what God has already ordained to be fulfilled by our foreknown prayers. Only God can change the course of events, but in any of the actions of Divine Governance, God has previously taken into account the prayers of His children and though certain things have been decreed to be from all eternity, the means of accomplishing them and the timing in history have been ordained to be dependent on the prayers of weak and fallible creatures. If evil appears to triumph, He is waiting for our prayer. If the course of action that we have pleaded seems to be at a standstill, He may be waiting for our dispositions to be changed as we pray in order that we be ready for His action when it comes . . ." for we do not know how to pray as we ought." (Romans 8:26)

We cannot reflect on this too much. Prayer has been ordained from all eternity to be an integral part of the Divine Government. What an immense privilege is ours in this call to commune with Almighty God and to take part in His own work.

> Prayer is not, in fact, a force having its first principle in us; it is not an effort of the human soul, trying to do violence to God in order to make Him change His providential dispositions. Such a manner of speaking, which is used occasionally, is a metaphorical, human way of expressing oneself. In reality, the will of God is absolutely immutable, but this superior immutability is precisely the source of the infallible efficacy of prayer.
>
> Fundamentally it is very simple in spite of the mystery of grace involved in it. We have here a combination of the clear and the obscure that is most captivating and beautiful. First of all, we shall consider what is clear: true prayer is infallibly efficacious because God, who cannot contradict Himself, has decreed that it should be. This is what the contemplation of the saints examines profoundly.
>
> Prayer is precisely a cause ordained to pro-

duce this effect: the obtaining of the gifts of God. (*The Three Ages of the Interior Life*, Garrigou-Lagrange, Vol. I, p. 431)

St. Gregory the Great says: "Men ought by prayer to dispose themselves to receive what Almighty God from eternity has decided to give them." (*Dialogues*, Bk. I, ch. 8)

In addition to this unspeakable truth is the fact that God Himself gives us the impulse to pray. As St. Paul says: "The Spirit prays in us with unspeakable groanings." (Romans 8:26)

Jesus Himself once said this to Sister Mary of the Trinity, a Poor Clare of Jerusalem:

> Did you hear your sisters say at recreation: "When one asks for suffering, that is a prayer that is sure to be answered?"
>
> When you ask for graces for souls, I grant them as infallibly as I do crosses, but they are less visible; and above all, do you understand that I grant you so many graces by which you benefit without even seeing them! You should say: "God answers every good and generous prayer."
>
> Oh, if you knew My thirst for souls and how much I Myself pray in you . . .! (*Spiritual Legacy of Sister Mary of the Trinity*, Newman, Westminster, Md., 1954, No. 447)

And elsewhere the Lord said to her:

> It is My joy to grant prayer. It is not a favor I confer on you alone. It is the same for every soul. Oh, if they understood! (Ibid., No. 131)

When we feel an ardent desire to pray for something, along with a great peace and an inner confidence, it is a sure sign that God wishes to grant our request and is Himself praying in us.

## III. PRAYER DEPENDS ON GOD'S SELF-REVELATION TO US AND OUR RESPONSE IN FAITH

All communion with God rests on His own revelation of Himself to us. Had He not taken the first step toward us in our sins, we would never be able to make that movement toward Him which is prayer. He shows us a glimmer of what He wants to do for us so that our hearts will desire and pray for it, just as a father opens his hands full of good things so that the children will ask for them. He is very disappointed if they do not want what he wants to give.

God wants very much to give us all we need, which is Himself, so He revealed Himself in glimpses, here and there, throughout the history of the people He first chose as the vehicle of His self-revelation. He manifested Himself as the Great God Who saved an undeserving and unworthy people simply because He wanted to. Because He wished to manifest His love, He saved them from the evil death toward which they were rushing heedlessly in the blindness of their ignorance.

He revealed Himself as the source of all temporal and spiritual blessings so that His people would come to Him in their needs. Gradually He tried to elevate their desires so that they would rise above the search for material concerns and recognize Him as their greatest and only need. He wanted to lift them to the level of thirst for Him alone, that is, to the level of perfect love and perfect desire. He does the same in each individual life, gradually educating us, through many sufferings, darknesses and trials, to the realization that He is above all, and greater than all the particular things we ask for. He is the substance of all we ask for, and He asks that we do not limit our desires by seeking what is less than the All. One day He said to Sister Mary of the Trinity:

> When you ask graces of Me for yourself or for others, your capacity for receiving is limited to your requests. When you await Me, asking for nothing but Myself, there is no limit in your heart. As soon as a soul awaits Me, I come to her. I have innumerable ways of approaching and speaking to her. . . . It is love that will make her discover My language. (*Spiritual Legacy of Sister Mary of the Trinity*, No. 140)

Loving desires are the wings that lift the soul to God and sustain its flight; when they begin to fail, fervor cools and the soul begins to fall and sink to a lower level of life. The beginning of all prayer is the desire to please God, to do His will and to become united with Him in doing so. Desire gathers all the faculties together and directs them to God and then, when they are so recollected and directed to Him, we are in the specific act of prayer.

The practice of prayer depends on keeping the soul and its faculties in constant pursuit of the contact with God; He feeds the hungry, but only the hungry. If we are always seeking to please Him, if we are always desiring Him, we will never be left alone without the food of His presence, as Jesus has said of Himself: "He Who sent Me is with Me and has not left Me alone because I always do the things that please Him." His will, His love, His presence are all one thing. To seek His will is to be in His presence, even when we do not feel anything. Prayer does not require any feeling of God. We may be arid, and distracted and have nothing to say to God but when we tell Him that, it becomes our prayer. This very humble effort will draw Him down to our poverty so that He will reveal Himself to us.

In prayer we feed our souls on God. The heavenly Father speaking to St. Catherine of Siena in the Dialogue on Prayer says:

> With exercise in perseverance, she (the soul) will taste prayer in truth, and the food of the Blood of My only-begotten Son, and therefore I told thee that some communicated virtually with the Body and Blood of Christ, although not sacramentally; that is, they communicate in the affection of charity, which they taste by means of holy prayer, little or much, according to the affection with which they pray. They who proceed with little prudence and without method, taste little, and they who proceed with much, taste much. For the more the soul tries to loosen her affection from herself, and fasten it in Me with the light of the intellect, the more she knows; and the more she loves, and, loving much, she tastes much. (*Dialogues*, Thorold, p. 165, Newman, 1943)

The same thought can be found in the *Imitation of Christ:*

> For he communicates mystically, and is invisibly fed, as often as he devoutly calls to mind the mystery of the Incarnation and Passion of Christ, and is inflamed with love of Him. (Bk. 4; ch. 10)

A mysterious and secret interior nourishment is given to the soul in prayer which, as it becomes stronger, flows out into all the activity. St. John of the Cross says that a mutual banquet is shared together by God and the person who loves Him, not only at prayer but throughout the day. This is, of course, a more advanced stage of prayer, but it is what we are preparing for and to sight the goal in the beginning draws us on in anticipation. Even in the beginning stages the mutual feeding of God on the soul and the soul on God begins to be experienced.

This inner food of God's Presence is given to those who do His will. It is really at this point that the words of Christ are fulfilled: "My food is to do the will of the Father." Through prayer we learn: "Not my will but Thine be done." When our will is one with His will the mutual contentment and refreshment of our soul in God is experienced. We must fix this truth deeply in our minds by often meditating on it. There is no such thing as communing with God unless we apply ourselves entirely to purity of conscience and the union of our wills with His. This is what St. Teresa says on the subject:

The highest perfection consists not in interior favours or in great raptures or in visions or in the spirit of prophecy, but in the bringing of our wills so closely into conformity with the will of God that, as soon as we realize He wills anything, we desire it ourselves with all our might, and take the bitter with the sweet, knowing that to be His Majesty's will. (*Book of Foundations*, ch. 5:10)

It is through the active efforts to conform our wills to God's will in obedience combined with the practice of recollection that the soul fits itself for prayer and gradually comes to taste how sweet the Lord is. But we must earn our own bread by using our minds to think of Him and our hearts to form loving affections until He begins to unveil His presence in the interior of our souls. This work of our minds and hearts is the constant return to the remembrance and consideration of the Incarnation and Passion of Christ as the above quotation of the *Imitation* remarks. Not only at formal times of prayer, but as often as we can, we must let our souls refresh themselves by bathing in the frequent recollection of the mystery of Jesus in Whom we live. Prayer is a dialogue with Him which flows from His revelation of Himself, and we enter into this mysterious self-revelation of God through His own gift of faith. Our present Holy Father Paul VI says that dialogue with God:

. . . Is the first and normal effect of the Gospel, of its light shining on a soul, which has opened to its rays. What do we call this projection of light? It is revelation. And what is this

opening of the soul? It is called faith. (General
Audience, 1/19/72)

## IV. RECOLLECTION AND THE PRACTICE OF THE PRESENCE OF GOD

The cultivation of this habit of frequently returning
to the remembrance of God or some mystery of the
Incarnation, has traditionally been called the practice
of the presence of God, although, strictly speaking,
we cannot really practice the presence of God since
God's presence is something given to us. God is
always present at all times and in all places. If He
gives a person a constant awareness of His presence,
it is a pure gift of grace, so that when we use this
term: "practice of the presence of God" we are
speaking of what we can do to train ourselves to
remember that He is with us in many different ways.
It refers to the use of our own God-given powers in a
special exercise that will develop a habit of seeing
Him everywhere and in every action, of looking to
Him for guidance, of being aware of Him here or
there, even when our minds are occupied, much the
same as a wife is constantly aware of her husband in
the room even while she is busy with her work. She
is not always thinking directly about him but she
speaks to him from time to time, or by a touch or
glance or smile maintains the warmth of their contact
and communion.

Every one of our thoughts cannot always be
directly on God. It is a matter of turning our minds
lovingly to Him whenever we can do so, so that

gradually we form a habit. A willingness and alertness to put out distractions is necessary. Gradually we come to abide in His love all the time and are able to be with Him without anxious strain to force our minds to think of Him constantly. Peace is always necessary to form this habit. All our efforts must be peaceful and gentle. We must not neglect to ask Him for the ability and grace to think of Him often and to stay with Him always. We must pray to be able to pray.

## A. The Presence of God Is the Key to the Spiritual Life and to Purity of Conscience

There are many different ways of recalling God's presence and of thus deepening our union with Him, but all of them must affect our conscience. The purpose of cultivating the habit of remembering God is that we will act according to His will. When we remember that He is here, all the powers of our souls are more easily gathered together and we are less vulnerable to the constant attacks of the evil one who would make us sin everywhere and in every circumstance, if he could. Living in God's presence is the answer to all our problems with the practice of virtue. If we lived always in His presence we would never sin.

The practice of the presence of God is the greatest aid to the fortification of the conscience and to the development of a sweet facility in surrendering ourselves totally to the good pleasure of God in everything that happens. This truth sounds very obvious but it can too easily be obscured. Some people have an extraordinary ease in remembering God or are habitually saying ejaculatory prayers and making aspirations, but show little correspondence when obedience requires that they submit their wills. For them, the practice of the presence of God is a mental exercise that one can develop as easily as one could acquire the habit of reciting the alphabet or the multiplication tables whenever one's mind was free from other things. In which case, this exercise, whatever it may be called, is not the practice of God's Presence which, if genuine, would change our entire life and all our attitudes and actions.

The *Imitation* gives us the prayer of the soul hungering for the presence of God and knowing that this is the fulfillment of every need:

> Behold, I stand before you poor and naked, begging Your grace, and imploring Your mercy. Feed Your hungry suppliant, inflame my coldness with the fire of Your love, enlighten my blindness with the brightness of Your presence. Turn for me all earthly things into bitterness, all things grievous and adverse into patience and all base and created things into contempt and oblivion. Lift up my heart to You in heaven and suffer me not to wander upon earth. May You alone be delightful to me from henceforth forevermore, for You alone are my meat and drink, my love and my joy, my sweetness and all my good. Oh, that with Your presence You would inflame, burn, and transform my soul into Yourself, that I may be made one spirit with You, by the grace of eternal union, and the melting of ardent love. Suffer me not to go from You hungry and thirsty, but deal with me in

Your mercy as You have often dealt wonderful-
ly with Your saints. What marvel if I should die
to myself; since You are a fire always burning
(Hebrews 12:29), and never failing; a love purifying the heart and enlightening the understanding. (Bk. IV, ch. 16:2, 3)

One of the most efficacious and most intelligent
means of developing an habitual contact with the
presence of God is to train ourselves to see Him
working in all the events of daily life, even the most
seemingly inconsequential details that appear to
happen by mere chance. Everything is arranged by
His providence for our good in order to provide us
with occasions of practicing and acquiring all the
various virtues; of detaching ourselves from our
own inordinate self-love and dependence on created
things and our all-too-human ways of judging. The
practice of the presence of God is a constant exercise
of faith. Once we come to recognize that it is the
Lord Who comes to us in the persons of the others,
that it is the Lord Who permits failure or
humiliation, success or benefit to come to us, we
have less difficulty in accepting and doing whatever
is required of us.

The eye of the mind and the eye of the soul are
not exactly the same thing; it is the eye of the soul we
must keep ever fixed upon the Lord. That means a
perpetual *disposition* to act whenever He wishes and
in whatever way He wishes, or not to act if that is
what He wishes. It means that gradually we come to
such an attunement to Him that we move with His
every movement just as a ballerina moves to every
subtle beat of the music, or a delicate harp vibrates
under the touch of a master artist. The eye of the

mind, that is, the mental exercise of reflection or conscious attention or remembrance, is a means of directing the eye of the soul and fixing it on the hands of the Lord, as Psalm 122 teaches us we must do. The hands of the Lord represent His action, the issuance of His orders and the indication of His desires. When our eyes are held there on Him, through the constant practice of a loving gaze ever ready to comply, then we have acquired the habit of the practice of the presence of God.

This first and most important means of developing a continual awareness of God is supported by the practice of conforming to Him our likes and dislikes, our views and opinions, our ways of regarding things and events. This means taking on the dispositions, attitudes and desires of Christ, or as St. Paul calls it, the Mind of Christ. If we only knew how easy it is to accustom ourselves to conforming our minds to His way of thinking, through love of Him, we would easily achieve this habit of remaining in His presence.

Not through strained efforts to meditate constantly on God but through a simplified abiding in love, watchful for every opportunity to surrender to the manifestations of His desires, does the soul come to the full union with Him. This was the way of the humble Carmelite lay Brother, Lawrence of the Resurrection, who has left us a most sure, attractive and efficacious means of dwelling always with God through love. He used his occupations as the object of his prayer during the day. He asked for God's help and companionship in all that he did. He adored Him there present with him. He praised and thanked Him for every pleasure and grace.

It was by fidelity in cultivating in his heart this deep presence of God, considered by faith, that Brother Lawrence began. He occupied himself with continual acts of adoration, love, invocation of the help of Our Lord in what he had to do. He thanked Him after having done it, he asked His pardon for his negligence, while confessing it, as he said, without making excuses to God. As these acts were so united to his occupations and the latter furnished him matter for them, he made them with the more ease. Thus, far from distracting him from his work, they helped him to do it well. (*The Practice of the Presence of God*, Brother Lawrence of the Resurrection, O.C.D.; Newman, Westminster, Md. 1952)

The time of action does not differ at all from that of prayer; I possess God as tranquilly in the bustle of my kitchen — where sometimes several people are asking me different things at one time — as if I were on my knees before the Blessed Sacrament. My faith sometimes even becomes so enlightened that I think I have lost it; it seems to me that the curtain of obscurity is drawn, that the endless, cloudless day of the other life is beginning to dawn. (Words of Brother Lawrence)

Brother Lawrence was faithful in rejecting every useless thought in order to occupy himself in the continual conversation with God until he reached a degree of union where the recollection of God was almost impossible to lose. He says that this presence is preserved rather by loving intercourse than by beautiful thoughts, understanding or intellectual meditations.

In the way of God, thoughts count for little, love does everything. And it is not necessary to have great things to do. I turn my little omelette in the pan for the love of God; when it is finished, if I have nothing to do, I prostrate myself on the ground and adore my God, Who gave me the grace to make it, after which I arise, more content than a king. When I cannot do anything else, it is enough for me to have lifted a straw from the earth for the love of God.

People seek for methods of learning to love God. They hope to arrive at it by I know not how many different practices; they take much trouble to remain in the presence of God in a quantity of ways. Is it not much shorter and more direct to do everything for the love of God, to make use of all the labors of one's state in life to show Him that, and to maintain His presence within us by this communion of our hearts with His? There is no finesse about it, one has only to do it generously and simply. (Ibid. p. 49)

His means of going to God was to do everything out of love for Him and so he was indifferent whether he was occupied with one thing or another, provided that he could do it for God and in obedience. It was God and not the particular means to Him that occupied his attention, and this is precisely the point of importance. We must not be concerned about the means of acquiring the presence of God, so that we are distracted by methods and constrained by tense unnaturalness in striving for a piety that is foreign to our inclinations. Brother Lawrence prayed everywhere, not using many words, but in the silence of the simplest acts of the soul where in work or rest, he praised and adored and thanked God continually. The application of his whole soul to God in all that he did made him gentle, affable, patient, obedient and charitable so that the practice of the presence of God was the source of all the virtues that began to take root in his soul. Through love he dwelt with the Lord although his natural life was still on earth, and being filled with God's presence he became detached from all that was not of God or for Him.

All that is excessive or defective in the soul is corrected, controlled and gentled by the application of the soul to the presence of God. As a person grows into the practice, he finds he has no need of calming himself because nothing in life throws him into excessive joy, sadness, anger or fear. The recollection of love keeps his interior powers in order. He does not become angry at the ignorance or even malice of others because he sees all in the providence of God and knows that God will rectify everything if he remains with Him as he should, in constant prayer. He does not become envious, because he has everything he wants in God. He does not love anyone excessively because he loves God and everyone for His sake. His soul becomes established in a firm and constant peace above all change, while he daily becomes more and more attached and rooted in the divine life. Thus is it clear that the constant return to the thought of God is the most fruitful and efficacious means of uniting our wills to His, of acquiring all the virtues and fulfilling the duties of our state of life.

This practice of remaining always in the presence of the Indwelling Trinity was also the dominating inspiration and influence in the development of the saintly life of Sister Elizabeth of the Trinity, a Carmelite nun who died at the age of twenty-six in the Carmel of Dijon, France in 1906. We have these precious passages from her letters:

> It seems to me that nothing can distract us from Him, if we are acting solely for Him, and remain always in His holy presence, while His divine gaze searches the very depths of our being: even in the midst of the world one can listen to Him in the silence of a heart that beats only for Him.
>
> Let us remain recollected in the presence of Him Who never changes, Who embraces us for ever in His love. We are "she who is not." Let us go to Him Who wants us to be entirely His and Who so penetrates us that it is no longer we who live, but He Who lives in us. (*Spiritual Writings*, Sister Elizabeth of the Trinity, edited by M.M. Philipon, O.P., Kenedy and Sons, N.Y. 1962 p. 31)

It is significant that the above two selections come from letters written while Elizabeth was still living in the world. Later from Carmel, she gives counsels to her mother for developing this intimate union in His presence:

> Profit by your solitude to recollect yourself with God. While your body is resting, think how He is the repose of your soul, and how, just as a child loves to rest in its mother's arms, so you can find repose in the arms of the God Who surrounds you on every side. We cannot depart from Him, but sometimes, alas! we forget His

holy presence and leave Him all alone while we concern ourselves with things apart from Him.

This intimate communion with God is so simple, it is restful rather than tiring, as a child remains at peace in its mother's presence. Offer Him all your sufferings; that is a prayer that is most pleasing to Him. (Ibid. p. 136)

Live with Him, I wish I could tell everyone what a source of strength and peace and happiness they would find, if they would consent to live in communion with Him. Only they don't know how to wait. If God does not give Himself to them in some perceptible way, they leave His holy Presence and when He comes to them laden with His gifts, He finds no one at home; they have gone out, occupied with exterior things; they do not dwell in the depths of their own being. (Ibid. p. 138)

## B. How Do We Attain To This Holy Recollection in God's Presence?

• First of all, we must have great sincerity of conscience. This does not mean absolute purity of conscience because we come to that purity of conscience only through remaining in God's presence. Continual prayer and purity of conscience are mutually interactive and they grow in direct proportion to each other. The preservation of the conscience rests on prayer and the converse is also true, there is no prayer without purity of conscience. If we are honest, any least trace of selfishness will bother us as soon as we kneel down to pray or strive to find God in our occupations. We cannot make protestations of love and fidelity to the Lord if we know we are not living up to them. Prayer is a real mirror of the soul. Perhaps not all at once, but sooner or later all the personal disorders will appear and have to be removed before there can be any progress.

To have intercourse with a wholly spiritual being does not require a great intellect or a lot of learning, but it does require a wholly spiritualized life, or at least the first steps toward attaining it, a sincere desire to persevere in acquiring it, and much practice at prayer itself. If we are weak in our daily decisions it is because we do not pray enough or remain in that loving recollection with God Who is a sun and a shield (Psalms 84:12) to the soul, instructing and enlightening the conscience. Or it is because we do not ask enough and with confidence for the graces we need in order to carry out what the light of God shows us we should do. Constant conversing with God in His living presence is the generator of the soul. It keeps the heat and blood circulating, the confidence and enthusiasm flowing. It keeps the eye of the soul clean to see God, and the desire enkindled to remain with Him.

• There must be a great fidelity to the practice of this loving recollection with God in faith. Fidelity depends on desire. If we really want something badly enough we will pay any price to have it. But this fidelity must be gentle, humble and loving, without giving in to trouble, anxiety or sadness when we fail to experience God or when we are unable to rise above our distractions and difficulties. Such distress often stems from an inordinate desire for success in experiencing God's sweet and consoling presence when He would be better pleased to let us feel and suffer the consequences of our own miseries for a while.

Prayer is an act of the soul, the mind and will, not a passing emotion. Some people yield to discouragement and abandon prayer thus turning away from the Lord when they do not feel His presence and are left without consolation. This is only self-seeking, not true love for Jesus, for if they sought Him alone, and persevered they would eventually come to enjoy His continual companionship. They would always have new lights, refreshment in Him and strength for whatever He asked of them.

Fidelity must be especially sustained through times of trial and suffering, in imitation of Jesus in the Garden. Prayer for Him then was an agony to accept the Father's will. One short prayer in suffering when we can do no better and when offered with submission and reverence, is more pleasing to Him and more efficacious for the whole Church than long hours of perfect recollection when we are full of consolation.

• There must be special care that this interior glance at God, however brief, precede and conclude every exterior action. From time to time we must look up at Him or simply pronounce His name lovingly. Time and effort is necessary to acquire this habit and we must not be discouraged when we fail. A habit is formed with effort through difficulties, but once it is acquired everything is done with ease and joy. St. Teresa of Jesus, speaking to her nuns says of this recollection:

> If she can, let her practice recollection many times daily; if not, let her do so occasionally. As

she grows accustomed to it, she will feel its benefits, either sooner or later. Once the Lord has granted it to her, she would not exchange it for any treasure.

Nothing, sisters, can be learned without a little trouble, so do, for the love of God, look upon any care which you take about this as well spent. I know that, with God's help, if you practice it for a year, or perhaps for only six months, you will be successful in attaining it. Think what a short time that is for acquiring so great a benefit, for you will be laying a good foundation, so that, if the Lord desires to raise you up to achieve great things, He will find you ready, because you will be close to Himself. May His Majesty never allow us to withdraw ourselves from His presence. (*Way of Perfection*, ch. 28:10)

This effort, a little burdensome and painful in the beginning, works its precious effects gradually. It draws down the rain of God's grace on the soul and, little by little brings it to that state of pure gazing or that loving sight of God in all things and everywhere, which is the most powerful, efficacious, and perfect form of prayer.

We must never think that our obligations or work, however absorbing they may be, or the unforeseen dispositions of providence or social obligations can of themselves be a hindrance to recollection. We must learn from the example of Jesus how our recollection can and must be maintained through everything and in the midst of everything. When a person has at last trained himself to keep his recollection, it becomes so natural that he preserves it without being aware of any effort and in such a manner that he scarcely ever departs from it.

In our society, preparation for one's occupation may take years of training and this for a short earthly existence. We should not expect to acquire the art of prayer immediately either, nor think it a waste of time and effort to really work at that which will be our occupation for eternity. To converse with God is our life's work as Christians.

We must continually purify our intentions and these frequent interior glances, accompanied by fervent aspirations of love, are like darts of heavenly fire which sweetly wound the Heart of Jesus and bring back to our own hearts the precious unctions of His grace. The saints teach us that this constant communion is a most efficacious means of arriving quickly at a high degree of holiness. These loving acts dispose the soul for an awareness of the touch of the Holy Spirit and prepare it for that loving infusion of God into the soul which we call contemplation. They arouse the ardor of charity so that it enfolds and penetrates all our works and keeps the soul in the presence of God. It is this constant activity of the heart and mind lifted up to Him that enables us to fulfill our Christian obligation to pray everywhere and always.

Perfect men never depart from this interior conversation except when the weakness of human nature and the alternations of time demand it, and even then, only for the briefest time for as soon as they advert to it they are again recollected. All their powers are spent in this activity without seeking or desiring anything other than to give place to the loving impulses of the divinity and to prepare themselves for God so that He may complete in them His most joyful operation. Without any other medium, the Heavenly Father can speak and produce words engendered by Him and bring His will to completion in every place, time and manner. (Tauler)

I cannot understand how religious persons can live content without the practice of the presence of God. As for me, I stay retired with Him in the depth and center of my soul as much as I can, and when I am thus with Him I fear nothing; but the least detour is a hell to me.

This exercise does not kill the body. Still, it is proper to deprive the latter from time to time, and even often, of many little consolations, although they are innocent and permissible; for God does not allow a soul that wishes to be entirely His to take its consolations elsewhere than with Him. That is more than reasonable.

I do not say that for this cause one should torment oneself. No, God must be served with holy freedom. We should labor faithfully, without trouble or anxiety, gently and calmly recalling our spirit to God as many times as we find it distracted from Him.

It is necessary, however, to place all our confidence in God and to rid ourselves of all other cares — even a quantity of special devotions, which although they may be good, have been undertaken rashly — since, after all, these devotions are only means to an end. So, when by this exercise of the presence of God we are with Him Who is our end, it is useless for us to return to the means. But we can continue our intercourse of love with Him, remaining in His holy presence; sometimes by an act of offering, or thanksgiving, and in all the ways that our spirit can invent.

Do not be discouraged by the repugnance that you may feel on the part of nature, for you must do violence to yourself. Often in the beginning we think the time is wasted, but we must continue and resolve to persevere in it until death and in spite of all difficulties. (*Practice of the Presence of God*, Brother Lawrence, Newman, 1952, letter 3)

God will reveal Himself, He is thirsting to do so, but He cannot unless the heart and mind are prepared to receive Him. Our life of prayer does not really begin until we have laid the foundations of a pure conscience, detachment, and the practice of remaining in His presence.

Frequently does He visit the internal man, sweet in His communication with him, delightful His consolation, much peace, and a familiarity exceedingly to be admired.

O faithful ṣoul, prepare your heart for this your Spouse, that He may vouchsafe to come to you, and dwell in you. (*Imitation*, Bk. II ch. 1, No. 1-2)

Why do you stand looking about you here, since this is not your resting place? Your dwelling must be in heaven and all things of the earth are only to be looked upon as passing by.

Let your thought be with the Most High, and your prayer directed to Christ without intermission. (Ibid. No. 4)

He to whom all things are known as they are, not as they are esteemed or said to be, is wise indeed, and taught rather by God than men.

He who knows how to walk interiorly, and to make little account of external things is not at a loss for proper places or times for performing devout exercises.

A spiritual man quickly recollects himself, because he never pours forth his whole self upon outward things.

Exterior labor is no prejudice to him, or any employment which for a time is necessary; but as things fall out, he accommodates himself to them.

If you had a right spirit within you and were well purified from earthly affections, all things would turn to your good and to your profit.

For this reason do many things displease and often trouble you, because you are not as yet perfectly dead to yourself, nor separated from all earthly things. (Ibid. No. 7-8)

Through recollection and the constant and total mortification of selfishness, we come to that much desired freedom which is so talked about in our age. True freedom is the freedom from selfishness. The habit of constant recollection and continual prayer in the presence of God is the remedy for that fear of dying to self and selfishness which is so ingrained in us. We cannot mortify ourselves without this spirit of habitual prayer. Prayer and self-denial are so inseparably linked that one cannot exist without the other. In prayer we experience the love of Jesus which lifts us up above all earthly things and gives a substantial freedom which is the mastery over self, until we are so free from self that we can even rejoice in contempt.

> If you had once perfectly entered into the interior of Jesus and experienced a little of His burning love, then you would not care at all for your own convenience, but would rather rejoice at reproach, because the love of Jesus makes a man despise himself.
>
> A lover of Jesus and of truth and a true internal man, that is free from inordinate affections, can freely turn himself to God and in spirit elevate himself above himself, and rest in enjoyment. (Ibid. No. 6)

By recollection and mortification we keep the Lord always with us as the *Imitation* says:

> It is a great art to know how to converse with Jesus, and to know how to keep Jesus is great wisdom. Be humble and peaceful and Jesus will be with you. Be devout and quiet and Jesus will stay with you. You may quickly drive away Jesus and lose His grace if you turn aside to outward things.
>
> Be pure and free interiorly, without being entangled by any creature. You must be naked and carry a pure heart to God, if you will attend at leisure and see how sweet the Lord is. (Bk. II, ch. 8:3, 5)

## V.  FORMS OF PRAYER

### A.  Vocal Prayer

God could easily read the depths of our souls and grant the unexpressed desires of our hearts and indeed He often does. He has no need that we express our prayers in words, but we have a need to do so. Vocal prayer is the outward expression of the inward sentiments which serves to fix these sentiments more deeply in our conscious minds, impress them on our hearts and memories and so draw the whole of our beings into our heart's most secret desires. Or rather we could say, vocal prayer helps to draw up the most intimate aspirations of our souls into our conscious exterior life. It helps us to realize our own interior thoughts and desires and it helps us to integrate our interior life of prayer into our exterior life of action. It helps to recollect our exterior faculties and draw them into the interior devotion of the soul.

Vocal prayer honors God not only with the soul and the inner sentiments but also with the body through word and action, and especially when we praise Him with His very own words in the Psalms and writings of Scripture. We sanctify our speech and our bodies when we speak His Word back to Him in prayer. God's Word effects a spontaneous combustion in the soul of the believer when it is spoken and heard with recollection and devotion. In the very act of speaking or listening to the living word, it works its effect in the soul. The speech of the Word is the infusion of the gift. In vocal prayer we receive new lights and the enkindling of new fervor which draw the soul into the interior and dispose it for the deeper recollection of silent interior prayer. St. Thomas says that vocal prayer "serves man that he may rouse himself by word of mouth to devout prayer." Simple observation of our own human nature teaches us that words and gestures intensify the acts of the heart and serve to pull together the scattered movements of our soul into one unified action.

In vocal prayer we offer God a sacrifice of praise, using our mouths to sing the songs of our hearts out loud. We thus repair for the numerous blasphemies uttered against Him by the demons and their human counterparts on earth, and perpetuate the Divine canticle of the Incarnate Word from the heart of the earth. In the Incarnation, celestial praise came down to earth so that the heavenly song of Infinite power, beauty and magnitude might arise from the depths of creation. In us, Christ continues His almighty work of thanking, praising, adoring, atoning and loving the Father in word and gesture, through our words and the ceremonial activity of the Church's liturgy. "Through Him, let us offer God an unending sacrifice of praise, a verbal sacrifice that is offered every time we acknowledge His name." (Hebrews 13:15) At the beginning of the Divine Office, the Church has placed this prayer:

O Lord, open my lips and my mouth shall declare your praise. O God, come to my assistance; O Lord, make haste to help me.

The Church is teaching us through these words to acknowledge that it is God Himself Who gives us the grace to praise Him verbally. We must depend on His powerful help to pay Him the homage of praise due Him. Vocal prayer is also a source of mutual encouragement, edification and the communication of fervor as we join together with others to give a united witness of our faith and gratitude to God and to profit from the support of the exterior faith and prayer of others. Greater fervor and strength are generated when we frequently come together to pray. Such has been the tradition of the Church in fidelity to the teaching of the Lord Himself Who promised that He would be present wherever two or three gathered in His Name wishing to profess their faith publicly.

To be well made, vocal prayer requires at least a few moments of quiet reflection and recollection on the dignity of the action and the One to Whom it is addressed — on the purpose, content and intentions of the prayer. We must strive to recollect ourselves as intensely as we can and refuse the admittance of useless and wandering thoughts, all the more so if the prayer is short, lest we find that it is over and done with, before we have even thought of what we were doing.

The frequent repetition of the same prayers over and over as years pass on, tends to dull us to their meaning. Too much familiarity tends to produce inattention unless we preserve our alertness by constant effort and continued renewal of frequently repeated acts of those virtues, intentions or aspirations found in each prayer. Fidelity to our required vocal prayer is a powerful help to the spirit of interior mental prayer, as well as a fruitful source of thoughts and aspirations that can be held quietly in the heart while their sweetness is extracted as one sucks a lemon drop or as a fragrant sachet penetrates precious linens. A single phrase of a Psalm or sacred text can flow through the mind and heart all day long, lifting up souls in song and bathing the mind in that precious living water of God's Word. Each time the Words of Scripture come to our reflection, they refresh the whole soul evoking sentiments of humble contrition, fervent desire, joyous gratitude or the sheer happiness of belonging to God and living in His Church all the days of our life.

Vocal and mental prayer permeate, sustain and assist each other. One cannot exist for long without the other, as St. Teresa says in Chapter 24 of the *Way of Perfection*, where she begins to explain the most perfect of all prayers, the Our Father.

She teaches us that we must stay close to the Master Who taught us His own prayer and exert all our efforts to learn the discipline of fixing our whole attention on Him.

> The Master is never so far away that the disciple needs to raise his voice in order to be heard: He is always right at his side. I want to have you understand that, if you are to recite the Pater Noster well, one thing is needful: you must not leave the side of the Master Who has taught it to you.
>
> You will say at once that this is meditation, and that you are not capable of it, and do not even wish to practice it, but you are content with vocal prayer. For there are impatient people who dislike giving themselves trouble, and it is troublesome at first to practise recollection of the mind when one has not made it a habit. So, in

order not to make themselves the least bit tired, they say they are incapable of anything but vocal prayer and do not know how to do anything further. *You are right to say that what we have described is mental prayer; but I assure you that I cannot distinguish it from vocal prayer faithfully recited with a realization of Who it is that we are addressing.*

O sisters, those of you whose minds cannot reason for long or whose thoughts cannot dwell upon God but are constantly wandering must at all costs form this blessed habit. I know quite well that you are capable of it— for many years I endured this trial of being unable to concentrate on one subject, and a very sore trial it is. But I know the Lord does not leave us so devoid of help that if we approach Him humbly and ask Him to be with us He will not grant our request. If a whole year passes without our obtaining what we ask, let us be prepared to try for longer. Let us never grudge time so well spent. Who, after all, is hurrying us? I am sure we can form this habit and strive to walk at the side of this true Master.

I am not asking you now to think of Him, or to form numerous conceptions of Him, or to make long and subtle meditations with your understanding. I am asking you only to look at Him. For who can prevent you from turning the eyes of your soul (just for a moment, if you can do no more) upon this Lord? . . . He is only waiting for us to look at Him, as He says to the Bride. If you want Him you will find Him. He longs so much for us to look at Him once more that it will not be for lack of effort on His part if we fail to do so.

. . . Little by little, persuasively and methodically, you will get your soul used to this, so that it will no longer be afraid of it. Remember that many years have passed since it went away from its Spouse, and it needs very careful handling before it will return home. We sinners are like that: we have accustomed our souls and minds to go after their own pleasures (or pains, it would be more correct to say) until the unfortunate soul no longer knows what it is doing. When that has happened, a good deal of skill is necessary before it can be inspired with enough love to make it stay at home; but unless we can gradually do that we shall accomplish nothing. (Ibid. ch. 26, Nos. 2, 3, 10)

## B. Mental Prayer

Mental prayer in my view, is nothing but friendly intercourse and frequent solitary converse with Him Who we know loves us. (*Life*, St. Teresa, ch. 8:5)

The soul's profit consists not in thinking much but in loving much. (St. Teresa, *Foundations*, ch. 5:2)

All prayer is a lifting up of the mind and heart to God. It is not so much an exercise of the mind in thinking, as a concentration of all the faculties through one single loving desire. In order to lift up our souls to Him we must prepare ourselves by making acts of acknowledgment that we are in His presence and humble ourselves as sinners before Him. We must believe in His love and willingness to hear us, we must hope to converse with Him and to be heard in our prayers, and we must love and adore Him.

Though we must strive to live in continual purity of heart in order to converse with God, the actual moments of prayer should also be preceded by special acts of contrition for our sins and petition to be clothed with His Own purity and holiness while we attempt to converse with Him. There is no better way to dispose ourselves to rise toward God, or rather to be lifted up by Him, than profoundly humbling ourselves before Him at the beginning of every prayer, no matter how brief. The Lord once gave St. Gertrude this instruction for a soul in her care:

Tell her from Me, that if she desires to unite herself to me by the tie of special love, she must, like a noble bird, make a nest at My feet of the branches of her nothingness and the palms of My greatness, where she may repose by a continual remembrance of her unworthiness . . . Let her often reflect on My mercy, and on the paternal goodness with which I am ready to receive men when they have fallen, if they return to Me by penance. When she desires to leave this nest in order to seek for food, she must fly into My bosom, wherein, with affectionate gratitude, she must reflect on the different blessings with which I have enriched her by My superabundant kindness. If she desires to fly further, and to ascend higher on the wings of her desires, she must rise with the swiftness of an eagle to the contemplation of heavenly things, which are above her; she must fly around My Face, supported like a seraph on the wings of charity, and gaze with the piercing eyes of her spirit upon the glory of the King of kings.

But since it is impossible for her during this

life to continue long in this high contemplation, even for an hour, she must depress her wings, by thinking frequently of her own nothingness, and return to her nest, remaining there in repose until she is able again to renew her flight by acts of thanksgiving and gratitude ... Thus by frequently repeating these difficult movements, entering into her nest by considerations of her unworthiness, and coming forth from it by meditating on My benefits, she will elevate herself to heavenly contemplation, and she will always taste celestial joys. (*Life and Revelations of St. Gertrude*, Newman, p. 270)

In symbolic language He teaches us those interior acts necessary to enter into and to persevere in prayer. We cannot rise to the state of supernatural contemplation by ourselves. The Lord Himself must lift the soul. However through constant repetition of the acts of humility, praise of His mercy and goodness, thanksgiving and petition, the soul is — little by little — disposed for the delicate action of God in lifting it up to Himself where it will experience the sweet and absorbing infusion of the divinity.

### • Meditation—The First Water

Meditation is the name given to that kind of interior activity wherein we use all the powers of our souls to reflect on some aspect of God, His creation, the Incarnation and Redemption. Meditation proceeds from point to point, considering relationships of truths and drawing conclusions, in order to evoke dispositions of humble contrition, thanks, praise, reparation and petition, so that we will be ready for His divine gift of contemplation when He wills to give it to us.

> . . . Mental prayer . . . consists in thinking of what we are saying, understanding it, and realizing Whom we are addressing, and who we are that are daring to address so great a Lord. To think of this and other similar things, such as how little we have served Him and how great is our obligation to serve Him, is mental prayer. (*Way of Perfection*, St. Teresa ch. 25:3)

In her *Life* and in the *Way of Perfection* St. Teresa speaks of the soul as a garden irrigated and kept alive by the waters of prayer:

> The beginner must think of himself as of one setting out to make a garden in which the Lord is to take His delight, yet in soil most unfruitful and full of weeds. His Majesty uproots the weeds and will set good plants in their stead. Let us suppose that this is already done — that a soul has resolved to practice prayer and has already begun to do so. We have now, by God's help, like good gardeners, to make these plants grow, and to water them carefully, so that they may not perish, but may produce flowers which shall send forth great fragrance to give refreshment to this Lord of ours so that He may often come into the garden to take His pleasure and have His delight among these virtues. (*Life*, ch. 11:6)

It is His Majesty Who uproots the weeds of our imperfections, sets the flower and fruit-bearing plants in the soil, and gives the water of prayer which alone can cause the growth of virtue. In the beginning we must labor for the water ourselves. Later on, God Himself gives the waters of prayer abundantly with very little effort on the soul's part:

> The beginner must consider how this garden can be watered, so that we may know what we have to do, what labour it will cost us, if the gain will outweigh the labour and for how long this labour must be borne. It seems to me that a garden can be watered in four ways: by taking the water from a well, which costs us great labour; or by a water-wheel and buckets, when the water is drawn by a windlass (I have sometimes drawn it in this way: it is less laborious than that other and gives more water); or by a stream or a brook, which waters the ground much better, for it saturates it more thoroughly and there is less need to water it often, so that the gardener's labour is much less; or by heavy rain, when the Lord waters it with no labour of ours, a way incomparably better than any of those which have been described. (Ibid. ch. 11:7)

We aspire to that stage where the Lord Himself will come and water our gardens with the overflow of His presence. This overflow of the Holy Spirit in our souls is God's free gift, yet we can and must do everything possible to prepare ourselves for it. We must labor diligently at our meditations and interior acts of virtue in order to water our souls with that water which St. Teresa says is drawn from the well by buckets.

And now I come to my point, which is the application of these four methods of watering by which the garden is to be kept fertile, for it will be ruined if it has no water.

Beginners in prayer, we may say, are those who draw up the water out of the well: this, as I have said, is a very laborious proceeding for it will fatigue them to keep their senses recollected, which is a great labour because they have been accustomed to a life of distraction. Beginners must accustom themselves to pay no heed to what they see or hear, and they must practise doing this during hours of prayer; they must be alone and in their solitude think over their past life — all of us, indeed, whether beginners or proficients, must do this frequently. There are differences, however, in the degree to which it must be done, as I shall show later. At first it causes distress, for beginners are not always sure that they have repented of their sins (though clearly they have, since they have so sincerely resolved to serve God). Then they have to endeavour to meditate upon the life of Christ and this fatigues their minds. Thus far we can make progress by ourselves — of course with the help of God, for without that, as is well known, we cannot think a single good thought. This is what is meant by beginning to draw up water from the well — and God grant there may be water in it! But that at least, does not depend on us: our task is to draw it up and to do what we can to water the flowers. (Ibid. ch. 11:8, 9)

To draw water from the well is to work with the understanding, imagination and memory in order to enkindle the will and start the flow of love which refreshes the soul. This is the first degree of prayer, that of beginners, and it is marked by effort and hard labor. Reflection and the concentrated application of an unruly mind is often as difficult as trying to ride a wild stallion. Many times distractions conquer us and there is no consolation to temper the dryness, boredom, darkness and repugnance in which the soul finds itself. But we must never give up. We must look to the good pleasure of the Master of the garden and not our own. St. Teresa says:

> It is in these early stages that their labour is hardest, for it is they themselves who labour and the Lord Who gives the increase. (*Life*, ch. 11:5)

He will eventually hear our prayer and grant the increase if we will persevere in ". . . lowering the bucket so often into the well and drawing it up without water."

But St. Teresa is not content with telling us about prayer and urging us on in our efforts, she also gives us sample forms of prayer so that we will know how to employ our time profitably:

> In this state it can *make many acts of resolution* to do great things for God and it *can awaken its own love.* It can make other acts which will help the virtues to grow . . . *The soul can picture itself in the presence of Christ,* and accustom itself to become enkindled with great love for His sacred Humanity and to have Him ever with it and speak with Him, *ask Him for the things it has need of, make complaints to Him of its trials, rejoice with Him in its joys* and yet never allow its joys to make it forgetful of Him. It has no need to think out set prayers but can use just such words as suit its desires and needs. This is an excellent way of making

progress, and of making it very quickly. If anyone strives always to have this precious companionship, makes good use of it, and really
learns to love this Lord to Whom we owe so
much, such a one, I think, has achieved a defi-
nite gain. (*Life*, ch. 12:2)

We can see that for St. Teresa mental prayer is
the means of drawing one's whole life into the life of
Christ. We talk to Him about our trials, we rejoice
with Him in our joys, we ask Him for whatever we
need, we try to keep Him with us all the time.
Gradually our entire existence becomes so bound up
with His life, thought, sentiments and desires that
we and Jesus are becoming knit together. Prayer then
begins to permeate the whole life because the Christ-
life is taking over our former life which centered
around ourselves.

The most efficacious of all meditations is the
frequent return to the Passion of the Lord so that we
may impress deeply on our minds and hearts the
depth and intensity of His love for us:

. . . We begin to meditate upon a scene of the
Passion — let us say upon the binding of the
Lord to the Column. The mind sets to work to
seek out the reasons which are to be found for
the great afflictions and distress which His
Majesty must have suffered when He was alone
there. It also meditates on the many other lessons which, if it is industrious, or well stored
with learning, this mystery can teach it. This
method should be the beginning, the middle and
the end of prayer for all of us: it is a most excellent and safe road until the Lord leads us to

other methods, which are supernatural. (*Life*, ch. 13:13)

> . . . It is well to reflect for a time and to think of the pains which He bore there, why He bore them, Who He is that bore them and with what love He suffered them. (Ibid. ch. 13:23)

It is in considering His deep wounds of love that Jesus teaches us secretly and mysteriously how to enter within them through contrition and humbled gratitude, as the *Imitation* tells us:

> . . . Rest on the passion of Christ, and willingly dwell in His sacred wounds, for if you flee devoutly to the wounds and precious stigmas of Jesus, you shall feel great comfort in tribulation; neither will you much regard being despised by men, but will easily bear up against detracting tongues. (Bk. II, ch. 1:4)

Resting in the wounds of Jesus, in confidence, abandonment and love, the soul begins to taste the fruit of her meditation in a quiet peace, in trust, in the joy of belonging to Him, in the inclination to the utter surrender of herself to the One Who redeemed her. It is through sharing His Passion with Him in prayer and in daily life that we begin to enter His risen life.

St. Teresa says that sometimes we are not able to think of the Passion, yet, we can remain quietly by the side of the suffering Lord compassionating Him and loving Him, sharing His interior dispositions through gentle acts of the soul made from time to time. This is called the Prayer of Recollection which will be explained in detail later.

But we must not always tire ourselves by going in search of such ideas; *we must sometimes remain by His side with our minds hushed in silence.* If we can, we should occupy ourselves in looking upon Him Who is looking at us; keep Him company; talk to Him; pray to Him, humble ourselves before Him; have our delight in Him; and remember that He never deserved to be there. Anyone who can do this, though he may be but a beginner in prayer, will derive great benefit from it, for this kind of prayer brings many benefits: at least, so my soul has found. (*Life*, ch. 13:23)

To remain by His side in silence is a particularly good form of prayer when the mind is fatigued. It well disposes the soul for contemplation. In fact, St. Teresa counsels us to learn how to *rest our souls in a peaceful gaze on the scene or mystery of Jesus* we have just used for our meditation, in order that we become accustomed to remaining with Him in quiet and surrendering our souls to an attitude of listening to whatever He would like to communicate to us. The worth of our prayer is measured more by how we listen to Him and His secret interior impulses to the soul, than by how successful, concentrated and distractionless the time of our meditation. The whole aim of prayer is to learn how to listen to God. The period of our meditation is simply to teach us how to do so and prepare us to receive the delicate inspirations of His grace which would be continuous if we would develop the habit of continuous listening. This very art of listening to God everywhere and always is contemplation itself and the goal toward which our beginning efforts of prayer are directed.

Returning, then, to those who can make use of their reasoning powers, I advise them not to spend all their time in doing so; their method of prayer is most meritorious, but enjoying it as they do, they fail to realize that they ought to have a kind of Sunday — that is to say, a period of rest from their labour. To stop working, they think, would be a loss of time, whereas my view is that this loss is a great gain; *let them imagine themselves, as I have suggested, in the presence of Christ, and let them remain in converse with Him, and delighting in Him, without wearying their minds or fatiguing themselves by composing speeches to Him,* but laying their needs before Him and acknowledging how right He is not to allow us to be in His presence. There is a time for one thing and a time for another; were there not, the soul would grow tired of always eating the same food. These foods are very pleasant and wholesome; and, if the palate is accustomed to their taste, they provide great sustenance for the life of the soul, and bring it many other benefits. (*Life*, ch. 13:12)

St. Teresa is teaching us that meditation is a means of collecting the soul in the presence of Christ, but once there, we must deliver our souls and all their faculties over to Him and enjoy His company as we would that of a beloved friend with whom we do not always feel the need of speaking. Once the contact with God is made through meditations and reflections we must not fear to allow ourselves just to remain there with Him in love, speaking to Him from time to time. This is the normal way for meditation to develop into a more simple form of prayer (called the Prayer of Recollection or Simplicity).

It can be compared to a bird in flight: at times it flaps its wings vigorously and at other times it soars in the wind carried on by the impetus of its former labor. But when it begins to sink, it once again returns to its own efforts to keep itself aloft. So the soul must return to meditation, reflection, or simplified acts of the various virtues when it begins to become distracted or the unction of love wanes. By alternately repeating these various acts of the mind, from meditation to affections to silent rest in His presence, then returning to meditation again when there is need, we keep our souls in flight and make steady progress toward the higher regions of prayer.

But there are many other subjects for meditation than the Sacred Passion which we need often to consider and allow to soak deeply into our minds and souls:

> . . . There will be many souls who derive greater benefits from other meditations than from that of the Sacred Passion. For, just as there are many mansions in Heaven, so there are many roads to them. Some people derive benefit from imagining themselves in hell; others, whom it distresses to think of hell, from imagining themselves in Heaven. Others meditate upon death. Some who are tender-hearted, get exhausted if they keep thinking about the Passion, but they derive great comfort and benefit from considering the power and greatness of God in

the creatures, and the love that He showed us, which is pictured in all things. This is an admirable procedure, provided one does not fail to meditate often upon the Passion and the life of Christ, which are, and have always been, the source of everything that is good. (*Life*, ch. 13:14)

It is true that some people are consistently drawn by an attraction to one or other of these subjects of meditation, but each of us will need to consider them all at one time or another. There will be periods and seasons in which we cannot think of anything but one certain aspect of the life of Jesus or Mary, or a particular attribute of God, or some article of the Creed, or perhaps all we can do, like St. Therese, is to say the Our Father or the Hail Mary, over and over again, quietly and slowly. Such is not without the Providence of God, Who may be attracting us to a special consideration which we particularly need in our present state of soul or because of some exterior condition of our life, and He wishes us to have a certain reflection of His own virtue or sentiments deeply impressed on our souls.

It may be that our temperament, or some indisposition, will not always allow us to think of the Passion, because of its painfulness; but what can prevent us from being with Him in His Resurrection Body, since we have Him so near us in the Sacrament, where He is already glorified? Here we shall not see Him wearied and broken in body, streaming with blood, exhausted by journeying, persecuted by those to whom He was doing such good, disbelieved by the Apostles. Certainly it is not always that one can bear to think of such great trials as those which He suffered. But here we can behold Him free from pain, full of glory, strengthening some, encouraging others, ere He ascends to the Heavens. In the Most Holy Sacrament He is our Companion and it would seem impossible for Him to leave us for a moment. (*Life*, St. Teresa, ch. 22:6)

The life and mysteries of Jesus are the sum total of all we need to nourish our souls. If we cannot seem to fit ourselves into one aspect of His life we can always find another to feed our meditations and affections. St. Teresa and St. John of the Cross are very insistent that we must always keep the Sacred Humanity before the eyes of our soul at every stage of the spiritual life:

It is a great thing for us, while we live as human beings, to have before us Christ's Humanity. (*Life*, St. Teresa, ch. 22:9)

Have the habitual desire to imitate Jesus Christ in all His works, conforming thyself to His life, whereon thou must meditate in order to imitate it and to behave in all things as He would behave. (St. John of the Cross, *Ascent of Mt. Carmel*, Bk. I, ch. 13)

The reason for this constant application of our soul's eye to the life and works of Jesus is that He is the only Way to the Father and our human nature needs a model:

As a rule, our thoughts must have something to lean upon, though sometimes the soul may go out from itself and very often may be so full of God that it will need no created thing to assist it in recollection. But this is not very usual; when we are busy, or suffering persecutions or at seasons of aridity, we have a very good Friend in Christ. We look at Him as a Man; we think of His moments of weakness and times of trial; and He becomes our Companion. Once we have made a habit of thinking of Him in this way, it becomes very easy to find Him at our side, though there will come times when it is impossible to do either the one thing or the other. (*Life*, St. Teresa, ch. 22:10)

It is not very usual that we find ourselves so full of God that we have no need to think of Christ to enkindle our souls, and this is especially true in the beginning of our life of prayer. Hence, we must apply ourselves with real diligence to acquiring this habit of bathing our distracted minds with the constant thought of Christ and His mysteries. The greatest help in doing so is the repeated use of the Scriptures, especially the Gospels through which Jesus has revealed Himself. Or we may take the mysteries of the Rosary and reflect on them with our Blessed Mother, contemplating their inner secrets and relishing their fruit. A good means is to think of these mysteries as taking place within us, as St. Teresa relates of her own early form of meditation:

I used to try to think of Jesus Christ, our Good and Loving Lord, as present within me, and it was in this way that I prayed. If I thought about any incident in His life, I would imagine it inwardly. . . . (*Life*, ch. 4:7)

There, within the shelter of our hearts, we can warm the shivering Infant with our love, we can repair for the rejection of others. We can feed and clothe Him with acts of faith, fidelity, trust in His goodness and love for us. We can heal His wounds with the balm of gratitude and appreciation. We can be Mary for Him in all His mysteries and conditions of life. We can surround Him with a globe of warmth as He suffered from the extreme cold in His flight into Egypt and atone for the coldness of so many hearts. We can be the silent womb of prayer that carries Him during Advent and the tomb in which He rests after His Passion. We can be the Heaven of delight in which He takes His joy at His Ascension as well as the companion of all His sorrows. We can be the Canaanite woman and the centurion who rejoiced Him by their faith and the beloved disciple who leaned on His Heart at the last supper.

We can be all things and everyone to Him in our prayer and find our whole recreation of soul in using our ingenuity to find ways of pleasing Him there. We can listen to the Sermon on the Mount and His instructions to the Apostles as though they were directed to us alone, or we can sit beside Him in the dungeon silently bearing His loneliness. We can be Mary with Him at home in Nazareth waiting on Him hand and foot and absorbing all His words. We can follow Him through forty days in the barren desert and learn how He prayed there. We can kneel beside Him in the Garden and unite our souls to His in agony over the loss of so many who will not come to Him.

The mysteries of Jesus and Mary are more ours

than theirs because they were lived for us by the Redeemer and His Co-Adjutrix, so that we could find in them strength, healing, grace and comfort for every need and state of soul we would ever pass through. For all the joys and trials of life we have a counterpart in the life of Jesus and Mary in which we can take refuge, drawing out all the grace we could possibly desire. We have the consolation of knowing that they lived through every possible life experience that could ever come to us and they did so precisely for us. Not only that, but the power and efficacious grace they merited for us is applied to our souls merely for the asking, as He has told us: "Ask and you shall receive." "Nothing is lacking to us of any grace," (I Corinthians 1:7), so we can "draw near with confidence to the throne of grace and find help in time of need." (Hebrews 4:16)

But His mysteries are not only ours in that we relate ourselves to them by means of meditation and impress their remembrance on our souls, nor even in that we partake of the grace coming from them and thus are able to practice the virtues required of us in comparable situations. His mysteries are ours especially in that, through prayer we become assimilated and transformed into Christ Himself Who gradually begins to take over all the movements and activity of our souls, so that Jesus Himself comes to live His very own life with all its mysteries in us. Then it is not we who live our own lives, practicing the virtues in imitation of Him through the meditation on His life, but rather Jesus Himself Who lives again under the accidents of our human characteristics. As in the Eucharist He is hidden under the veil of the bread and wine, so in us

He is hidden under the veil of our particular name and history and appearance and personality, with all our faults and failings and very human defects. This transformation is the mystery of Jesus.

One of the best means of facilitating this transformation into Jesus through a deep penetration into the dispositions of His soul, is the meditation on the Psalms. It has been said that the Gospels give us the account of His life and works and the Psalms reveal to us the sentiments of His inmost heart. They give us the soul of Jesus. We can take a single Psalm, such as Psalm 69 (68) where we find the soul of the Savior overwhelmed by floods of suffering, like deep waters rushing up to engulf Him, and let the same feelings and thoughts of His heart flow into our own.

> Save me, God! The water is already up to my neck! I am sinking into the deepest swamp, there is no foothold; I have stepped into deep water and the waves are washing over me. Worn out with calling, my throat is hoarse, my eyes are strained looking for my God.
>
> More people hate me for no reason than I have hairs on my head, more are groundlessly hostile than I have hair to show.
>
> \*     \*     \*
>
> It is for you I am putting up with insults that cover me with shame, that make me a stranger to my brothers, an alien to my mother's other sons; zeal for your house devours me, and the insults of those who insult you fall on me.
>
> For my part, I pray to you, Yahweh, at the time you wish; in your great love, answer me, God, faithful in saving power.
>
> \*     \*     \*

You know all the insults I endure, every one of my oppressors is known to you; the insults have broken my heart, my shame and disgrace are past cure.

I had hoped for sympathy, but in vain, I found no one to console me. They gave me poison instead, when I was thirsty they gave me vinegar to drink.

In the bitterness of His sorrowful loneliness we can join the loneliness of our own lives and be to Him now the consoler that He could not find in the hour of His Passion. Or we can find His soul in the joy of the Resurrection and exult with Him in His glory:

So my heart exults, my very soul rejoices, my body, too, will rest securely, for you will not abandon my soul to Sheol, nor allow the one you love to see the Pit; you will reveal the path of life to me, give me unbounded joy in your presence, and at your right hand everlasting pleasures. (Psalm 16 [15]: 9-11)

With the help of a good commentary on the Psalms and with a thoughtful reading of each verse we will be prepared for a most fruitful hour of prayer which will help to draw us more deeply into the innermost thoughts of Christ. Gradually we come to live the Psalms we say each day in the very Person of the Redeemer, through the union of mind and heart with Him which has grown in our mental prayer. We come to put on His mind, as St. Paul instructs us (Philippians 2:5), so that we can praise the Father in the soul of Jesus. We can extend the power of His intercession to the ends of the earth and penetrate every open heart with the efficacious grace streaming from the infinite prayer of Christ Who is now praying within us.

### • The Carmelite Method of Meditation

The purpose of a method of meditation is to serve as a scaffolding or framework for the building we wish to erect. Without at least some very simple outline of prayer we do not know what to do, and we run the risk of wandering aimlessly about with little or no profit. A method is necessary to utilize the time well in order that we may attain our goal of really praying; to prevent prayer from degenerating into mere day-dreaming and useless rumination; to support us in times of aridity, temptation and darkness; and to be a firm foundation for a real Christian formation. If we wish to live a Christian life of prayer we must expect to be formed in prayer and by means of prayer. Beginners should learn a traditional and flexible method of prayer and exercise themselves faithfully in it until God leads them to another simpler form of prayer.

From what has already been said about the practice of the presence of God, the habit of general recollection, it is evident that prayer is not a time of speculation on religious truths, nor a good opportunity to develop our theological insights, nor to get our practical thinking or moral problems done. We use our minds just enough to consider some truth of faith which will bring us into direct contact with God and stir up the fire of love, which will in turn motivate our entire lives toward the imitation of Jesus.

Prayer is not an intellectual reflection on a spiritual subject, nor a good little sermon that we preach to ourselves, no matter how apt it may be, or how much we need that exhortation. Nor is it an examination of conscience or a time to study passages of Scripture or some other religious writer that we particularly like. Prayer is not a work of the intellect deducing conclusions and finally formulating moral resolutions, though almost all of the above mentioned may be a part of prayer or may be utilized during prayer to stimulate prayer.

Prayer, above all, is a loving conversation or communion with God. Perhaps communion is the better word, since conversation connotes an exchange of words and thoughts, whereas one can commune with another entirely in silence. We must become used to this latter idea of prayer as the goal of prayer toward which we are striving, since contemplation, toward which meditation leads, is a very simple, silent communion with God through Love. In the words of St. Teresa:

> I only want you to be warned that, if you would progress a long way on this road and ascend to the Mansions of your desire, the *important thing is not to think much, but to love much; do then, whatever most arouses you to love.* Perhaps we do not know what love is: it would not surprise me a great deal to learn this, for love consists, not in the extent of our happiness, but in the firmness of our determination to try to please God in everything, and to endeavour, in all possible ways, not to offend Him, and to pray Him ever to advance the honour and glory of His Son and the growth of the Catholic

Church. Those are the signs of love; do not imagine that the important thing is never to be thinking of anything else and that if your mind becomes slightly distracted all is lost. (*Interior Castle*, IV, ch. 1:8)

To love Him is to be determined to please Him in everything and not to offend Him in anything. That means complete conversion of soul, so that we come to live only for His glory. This is the test of how genuine our prayer life is and the measure of any particular hour of prayer. We may be beset with many distractions, but if we find that, no matter what comes, we are growing more and more determined to live only for Him and to please Him in each action of the day, however inconsequential it may be, then, our prayer is real prayer.

The soul's profit, then, consists not in thinking much but in loving much. How shall this love be acquired? By our resolving to work and to suffer and by our doing so whenever the occasion offers. It is very true that by thinking what we owe the Lord, and Who He is, and what we are, a soul will be led to make such a resolution. To do this is a great merit and very fitting for beginners. . . . (St. Teresa, *Foundations*, ch. 5:2-3)

Yes, love for God does not consist in shedding tears, in enjoying those consolations and that tenderness which for the most part we desire and in which we find comfort, but in serving Him with righteousness, fortitude of soul and humility. (*Life*, St. Teresa, ch. 11:14)

This love is His and comes from Him. It is chiefly for this love that we pray. From the beginning to the end of our life it must permeate all our thoughts and meditations, all our means and methods, all our practices and devotions, or our prayer will be nothing and our virtue sheer illusion.

> . . . Love begets love. And though we may be only beginners, and very wicked, let us strive ever to bear this in mind and awaken our own love, for, if once the Lord grants us the favour of implanting His love in our hearts everything will be easy for us and we shall get things done in a very short time and with very little labour. May His Majesty give us this love, since He knows how much we need it, for the sake of the love which He bore us and through His glorious Son, Who revealed it to us at such great cost to Himself. Amen. (*Life*, *St. Teresa*, ch. 22:14)

This method of mental prayer teaches us to reflect on some truth long enough to stir our affections. It teaches us to rest for a time in a loving possession or a loving gaze (contemplation) on the truth we have considered and to finish our prayer with acts of thanksgiving, offering ourselves to His service and asking for all our needs. Reasoning is subordinated to affective prayer in all true methods of prayer. This method aims at disposing the soul to contemplation as quickly as possible. St. John of the Cross states this clearly in the *Ascent of Mt. Carmel*, Book II:

> Meditation is ordered to contemplation as to its end.

It should be known that the purpose of discursive meditation on divine subjects is the acquisition of some knowledge and love of God.
(ch. 14:2)

The method, then, in brief outline is:

• Remote preparation: the habitual practice of
recollection and the presence of God.

• Proximate preparation: the reading of some
spiritual book suited for prayer.

• The meditation proper.

• Colloquy or loving conversation with the
Lord.

• Thanksgiving.

• Oblation of ourselves in union with Christ
the Divine Victim.

• Petition for our needs, for souls, for the
Church.

The remote preparation has already been
explained in the beginning when we spoke of the
obligation to live continually in the presence of God.
If we spend the entire day in a loving dialogue with
Him, in the manner described by Brother Lawrence
and St. Teresa, we will have no difficulty when the
time for prayer comes. We will be able to adjust our
minds from our work to the concentrated application
of prayer; that is to say, usually, because there are
always unforeseen exterior and interior causes which
will intervene to distract us and make prayer
difficult, and not without the providence of God
Who sometimes wants us to struggle a little before
He gives us the grace of prayer.

The reading we do in order to immediately
dispose our minds for prayer is of vital importance;

it should be done slowly and with reflection. Where particular thoughts especially strike us, we should interrupt our reading to allow the inspiration time enough to sink more deeply in our minds. We need not use all the thoughts that we have prepared for our time of prayer, it is better to have an abundance rather than not enough and should we run dry, we must have the book at hand so that we can refresh our thoughts and repel distractions.

This preparation for prayer is most important since, as our preparation is, so will our prayer be. Very often the distractions and aridity we complain of may be the result of a lack of earnest preparation and sincere petition for the *actual grace* needed to begin the act of prayer. In the Scriptures, especially the Gospels and Psalms, we have the most fruitful source of meditation since these are God's own Words to us. However, there are times when we cannot seem to get any light or help from Scripture. At such times it is a help to use something which will lead us to Scripture by explaining it directly or indirectly, by showing us how to read it, how to interpret it, and how to understand the lessons of Jesus as they are to be lived in our particular life.

The meditation itself should begin with an acknowledgment that we are poor sinners coming into the presence of the Divine Majesty. Some kind of examination of conscience, even though it be brief, is necessary in order that any still unrecognized or unrepented faults and sins will be removed before we attempt to converse with the All Holy One. The heart must be pure or we will not be able to pray. If there is an obstacle or anything we are secretly covering up or trying to hide from ourselves, the eye of the soul will keep returning to that stain on the conscience during the time of prayer, until we face it in front of Him. He will not permit an interview with Him in the presence of insincerity, or a careless negligence in purifying our hearts.

> As you know, the first things must be examination of the conscience, confession of sin and the signing of yourself with the Cross. Then daughters, as you are alone, you must look for a companion — and Who could be a better Companion than the very Master Who taught you the prayer you are about to say? (*Way of Perfection*, ch. 26:1)

Here St. Teresa is teaching us how to pray the Our Father as the norm and chief of all meditations. She says that having examined our conscience and humbled ourselves, we must seek the presence and companionship of the Lord Who will Himself teach us to pray. It is a good practice to begin every hour of prayer with the Our Father.

Meditation may be of an intellectual type without any imaginary representation to initiate it, or it may be an imaginary-intellectual meditation begun with the aid of images represented to the mind. This imaginary representation should always be brief, that is, only as long and as much as is necessary to fix the ideas in the thoughts and to inspire the consideration of them. If the imagination is allowed to dwell too fixedly on the images formed we are in danger of falling into an illusion of spending a great deal of time in the images and enjoying them for themselves and then thinking we have prayed when we have spent most of the hour making lovely pictures and mistaking the image for the reality.

All of us, especially those with lively imaginations, should avoid detailed picture-making or a multiplicity of images. The representation should be made moderately and only inasmuch as it helps to gather our thoughts together and give us material to think about. Once the Person of Jesus or Mary, some aspect of their lives, or some other suitable subject is placed before our minds we should attempt to leave the use of the image as quickly as possible because the corporeal and particular image is only a stepping-stone to the spiritual and universal thought. St. John of the Cross tells us in the *Ascent of Mt. Carmel* that:

> Nothing which could possibly be imagined or comprehended in this life can be a proximate means of union with God.
>
> It is noteworthy that among all creatures both superior and inferior none bears a likeness to God's being or unites proximately with Him. Though truly, as theologians say, all creatures carry with them a certain relationship to God and a trace of Him (greater or less according to the perfection of their being) yet God has no relation or essential likeness to them. Rather the difference which lies between His divine being and their being is infinite. Consequently, intellectual comprehension of God through heavenly or earthly creatures is impossible, since there is no proportion of likeness. (Book II, ch. 8:3-4)

We can gather from what has been said that to be prepared for this divine union the intellect must be cleansed and emptied of everything relating to sense, divested and liberated of everything clearly apprehensible, inwardly pacified and silenced, and supported by faith alone, which is the only proximate and proportionate means to union with God. For the likeness between faith and God is so close that no other difference exists than that between believing in God and seeing Him . . . *Only by means of faith, in divine light exceeding all understanding, does God manifest Himself to the soul. The more intense a man's faith, the closer is his union with God.* (Ibid., ch. 9:1)

Since it is by means of faith that we touch God and hold on to Him, *we must learn how to converse* with Him *in faith* from the very beginning of our life of prayer. Therefore, we must use created things, including our own interior powers of imagination, memory, intelligence, only inasmuch as they serve to elicit acts of faith and enkindle love in the will. Our meditations are only as good as they are full of faith, hope and charity. Like swimmers learning to use their arms and legs in unified movements in order to pass smoothly and swiftly through the water, so we, in prayer learn to use our faculties in unison to head for the deep waters of faith.

Once we have sufficiently represented our subject and impressed it on our minds, we consider the truth more thoroughly in order to move the will to acts of love and instigate a living conversation with Him. The goodness and love of God for us must be the beginning and end of all our considerations, and we consider it to become more convinced of it. All that we meditate upon should be related to this beginning and end of all things: God's goodness. We have already quoted passages of St. Teresa in which she gives us samples of how the soul proceeds in this second step of the meditation. It ponders for example: the greatness and mercy of the Son of God Who wished to suffer such terrible things for those who had offended Him; the love and sweetness with which He suffered and pardoned His executioners; His great dignity contrasted with the ignominious characters who were the object of His mercy; the great malice of sin which necessitated such expiation.

In these two first parts of mental prayer, that is, the representation and the consideration, the soul is prepared and disposed to pray and converse with God, but in order to actually do so, it must pass on to the third step, otherwise it would still only be conversing with itself. It is in this third part of prayer, the colloquy, that one really speaks to God, that one really prays. The colloquy or loving conversation leads to contemplation.

It is possible to consider the most beautiful and inspiring religious truths and yet remain dry and untouched by them because we have not made contact with the God Who is their very source present within us. We must turn our thoughts within and by faith embrace Him with mind and heart, knowing that whatever subject we have just pondered is contained within us in its fullness because we possess it all in Him. Here we speak to Him, rejoice in His presence, ask Him for what we need or just remain silent with Him listening to whatever He wishes to say to us. "Do you suppose He is silent, though we cannot hear Him? He speaks to our hearts when our hearts speak to Him." (*Way of Perfection* 24:4)

We should not expect clearly articulated words but rather the inspirations of grace formed by the Holy Spirit in the mind and the movements or inclinations of grace aroused in the will and affections. God enlightens the mind *according to what it has just considered.* Greater insights into an already known truth are given and greater firmness of conviction is formed in the will. By an illustration of clearness God impresses truth on the soul in silence and thus we say He speaks to the soul, or inspires it, that is, breathes into it. It is in these moments of prayer that we find St. Teresa's definition of prayer in its living reality, for *this is* the intimate communion with God Who we know loves us.

Having found Him by its reflections, the soul now pours out her loving affections, but should these affections become too ardent for a prolonged period, one should gently temper them and even turn the mind away to other religious thoughts in order to give the soul a little rest. The reason is that here, the emotions of the soul are not yet purified and ardor of soul, though very good, is not in this state free from excess. Even affections given and stimulated by God can become excessive so that the soul is carried away by sensible fervor, not only at the time of prayer, but often throughout the day. The joy and consolation experienced here are still chiefly of the sensible kind and are apt to be indulged in by the soul. If so, the result will be a plunge into aridity as soon as the fervor dies down.

If we let ourselves go, so to speak, in the affections of sensible love, before long we allow ourselves excessive joy in the experience, we become too free with ourselves, too elated with the consolation of it, too over-confident in what we think is pure Divine love. It can be purely emotional experience that we surrender to and before long we find that we have lost control of ourselves and fallen into faults which jolt us back into reality again. If we place no restraint on our affections and just let ourselves "fly off the handle," as the saying goes, we will hurt our souls and then have to suffer the consequences of ensuing dryness and desolation, feelings of disgruntled irritability, clouding of the senses, and sensible dissatisfaction for perhaps hours afterward, until we have paid the little debt to Divine justice in suffering the *natural effects* of inordinate indulgence in our emotions, even those of the highest purpose.

Here, true fervor for the things of God is so mixed with human nature's yet very strong inclinations of inordinate emotion or passion and the effects of original sin that we must exercise careful vigilance and restraint upon ourselves even in the exercise of our love for God. It needs to be enkindled and kept at a steady heat, but we must watch it closely, mortify ourselves and gentle it by control, just as we guard and control a fire needed to warm the house, but well kept in the furnace.

This colloquy is the center and most important point of prayer. Everything preceding it has led up to it, and that which is to follow will continue and complete it. Once having found the loving Lord within our own hearts and been privileged to converse with Him, we instinctively pour forth praise and thanksgiving. We offer ourselves to Him as some small means to requite such love, and we ask the necessary graces to continue in this love. Thus we can see that the colloquy is the essence of prayer and the only absolutely necessary part. The other parts are only subsidiary. Some might be left out entirely, such as the reading or the representation which may not be necessary at times. The last three steps may be part of the colloquy.

It may even be that we are frequently able to begin the colloquy as soon as we enter prayer and the whole of it becomes an alternation of acts of praise, love, gratitude, silence, petition, etc. Or perhaps all these steps of the method may be used in a form such as this: the reading of a simple sentence or a single thought and a little conversation with Him about it, accompanied by acts of love, petition, etc., continued as long as the soul is nourished by them. Then, perhaps we will need to pass back to the same thought again or to read a new one, and the same process is repeated following successive related thoughts as the soul has need. The soul, as it were, takes a little bite, chews, enjoys and swallows it, then takes another, as slowly and deliberately as it finds helpful. Some days we might feel attracted to spending the entire period of prayer in praise and thanksgiving and we find our hearts pouring out the words of the Gloria or the Magnificat. At other times we may not find that praise, or anything else, comes so spontaneously, but we can spend the time slowly repeating the Gloria or the Creed or some Psalm, quietly relishing the phrases in the presence of the

Lord and making each word an arrow of love to pierce His Heart.

Thanksgiving. We can go through all the benefits of the redemption and all the personal gifts and graces of our lives, thanking Him for each, one by one. We thank Him for the privilege of being able to spend an hour of prayer with Him and for being called to live the Christian life. Gratitude is the surest way to open our souls to the fullness of the benefits which He wishes to give because gratitude is so closely allied to humility.

The offering. The greatest proof of love is to give oneself to the beloved totally and unreservedly. The surrender of ourselves and everything we have into the hands of God so that He may dispose of us as He wills is the beginning and end of all holiness. Until we abandon ourselves to Him entirely with no other private desires outside of His will for us there is no such thing as attempting to converse with Him in the intimate union of prayer. All our temporal and spiritual concerns must be placed confidently in Him and we must renew that offering each day, in fact, it may be necessary to do so many times a day and in detail, in order that it may be deeply impressed on our minds and actually influence our thoughts and behavior in moments when we feel contrary forces pulling against our commitment to God. Therefore, we cultivate the habit of renewing our offering at the end of each hour of mental prayer, after contemplating His overwhelming love for us, hoping that our offering will become more and more pure, ardent and intense every time we make it, so that we may become increasingly His. It may often be helpful to make a detailed offering of each action we will do this day: of our soul and all its powers and interior movements; our desires and intentions, fears and cares; our loved ones, our health, life, duties, honors and failures or whatever may be especially on our minds at this present moment of life, remembering St. Teresa's words:

> The important point is that we should be absolutely resolved to give it (our soul) to Him for His own and should empty it so that He may take out and put in just what He likes, as He would with something of His own. His Majesty is right in demanding this; let us not deny it to Him. And, as He refuses to force our wills, *He takes what we give Him but does not give Himself wholly until He sees that we are giving ourselves wholly to Him.* This is certain, and, as it is of such importance, I often remind you of it. *Nor does He work within the soul as He does when it is wholly His and keeps nothing back.* (*Way of Perfection*, ch. 28:12)

The Petition. He desires that we ask Him for all that we need, even though He knows that better than we do, and when we ask, He always gives more than we ask. The subject of our prayer will inspire our requests. If, for example, we have meditated on His Passion, we will realize our need for His patience in our own sufferings and trials, for His meekness and sweetness in dealing with those who try us. We will ask for His own love so that we can repay His love for us. We will ask for all the necessities of our own souls and of all those near and dear to us. We will feel our hearts being expanded to the dimensions of the entire universe and ask for the salvation of each and every soul on earth, especially the Church, priests and the chosen ones of God. We must never be afraid of asking too much, for the more we ask Him the more lavish He is in giving. Great requests come out of great confidence. Those who distrust Him are afraid to ask too much. They measure Him by their own degree of generosity. But His children ask much because they know their Father's Heart; they know how much He has to give and how much He desires to give. It is this confidence itself which pleases Him and opens the floodgates of grace. Confidence can obtain anything from His Heart as He said to Sister Mary of the Trinity:

> I cannot resist those who ask with humility. I always end by yielding to those who ask with perseverance. To those who ask with love, that is to say, with unlimited confidence, I cannot prevent Myself from granting even more, far more than what is asked.
>
> It is not what you give Me that glorifies Me, it is when, by your confidence, you give Me the opportunity of showing you what My love is capable of devising for you. . . . (*Spiritual Legacy of Sister Mary of the Trinity;* Nos. 217, 161)

The spirit of confidence, joined with true abandonment to His will and the purity of a heart which is sincere with Him, reverent and determined to use the grace it asks for, combine to make all-powerful prayer which will assuredly obtain all it asks.

## C. The Prayer of Recollection or Simplicity

The Prayer of Recollection is sometimes called the Prayer of Simplicity, or simplified affective prayer, or the prayer of simple regard. As the name suggests, it is a more simplified form of prayer advancing beyond discursive meditation (discursive meaning that the faculties of the soul, chiefly the intellect, discourse and reason and consider the subject of the meditation, advancing from conclusion to conclusion in order to arrive at the affective colloquy). In the Prayer of Recollection the soul bypasses the discourse and quickly but simply gathers together all the powers of the soul within itself. This prayer is a quieting of the mind which, after having developed habits of meditation and considerations of truths of God and His mysteries, can now "hold" these truths simply in itself, loving quietly. As yet, it is *not infused* recollection, which is the beginning stage of contemplation, but the preparatory stage preceding and disposing the soul's natural activity to receive infused prayer. At first this quiet repose in the truth formerly meditated upon, lasts for only a few brief moments and then yields to other thoughts and affections, since, by our own natural efforts, we cannot keep our minds quiet for long.

> It is only little by little that the soul becomes accustomed to look at and to love God Himself by a simple view of faith for a notable period of time, much as the artist contemplates his master-piece, the details and elements of which he had previously studied. It seems indeed that here

there takes place an ordinary psychological process which evidently presupposes a live faith, and even the hidden action of the Holy Ghost, but not a special intervention of God." (*The Spiritual Life*, Tanquerey, p. 646)

St. Teresa gives a description of this prayer as it comes *after a meditation:*

*Meditation:* ... upon Christ bound to the Column — it is well *to reflect* for a time and *to think of the pains which He bore there, why He bore them, Who He is that bore them* and *with what love He suffered them.* But we must not always tire ourselves by going in search of such ideas; *Prayer of Recollection: ... we must sometimes remain by His side with our minds hushed in silence.* If we can, we should *occupy ourselves in looking upon Him* Who is looking at us; keep Him company; talk with Him; pray to Him; humble ourselves before Him; *have our delight in Him;* and remember that He never deserved to be there. (*Life*, ch. 13:23)

She says that the soul by its own effort withdraws within itself, into its own little interior heaven to find God and remain there with Him alone.

... The soul collects together all the faculties and enters within itself to be with its God. Its Divine Master comes more speedily to teach it, and to grant it the Prayer of Quiet, than in any other way. For, hidden there within itself, it can think about the Passion, and picture the Son, and offer Him to the Father, without wearying

87

the mind by going to seek Him on Mount Calvary, or in the Garden, or at the Column. (*Way of Perfection*, ch. 28:5)

St. Teresa makes it clear that the soul must exert its own effort to recollect itself and turn its attention toward the Indwelling God and that it has the power to do so if it will exercise itself in restraining the exterior senses and directing the gaze of the soul within:

> . . . We must recollect our outward senses, take charge of them ourselves and give them something which will occupy them. It is in this way that we have heaven within ourselves since the Lord of Heaven is there. (Ibid., ch. 23:6)

> . . . I should like to be able to explain the nature of this holy companionship with our great Companion, the Holiest of the holy, in which there is nothing to hinder the soul and her Spouse from remaining alone together, when the soul desires to enter within herself, to shut the door behind her so as to keep out all that is worldly and to dwell in that Paradise with her God. I say "desires," because you must understand that *this is not a supernatural state but depends upon our volition, and that, by God's favour, we can enter it of our own accord. . . . For this is not a silence of the faculties: it is a shutting-up of the faculties within itself by the soul.*
> There are many ways in which we can gradually acquire this habit, as various books tell us. We must cast aside everything else, they say, in order to approach God inwardly and we must

retire within ourselves even during our ordinary occupations. If I can recall the companionship which I have within my soul for as much as a moment, that is of great utility. (Ibid., ch. 29:4-5)

The *general habit* of recollection that we practice throughout the day is the greatest help to this *Prayer* of Recollection, but we must know that there is a distinction between them. We could not constantly keep ourselves in the intensity of the *Prayer of Recollection* all day long, since we need to attend to other things, but St. Teresa tells us what to do during our ordinary occupations in order to facilitate the rapid acquisition of this method of prayer:

> I conclude by advising anyone who wishes to acquire it (since as I say, it is in our power to do so) not to grow weary of trying to get used to the method which has been described, for it is equivalent to a gradual gaining of the mastery over herself and is not vain labour. *To conquer oneself for one's own good is to make use of the senses in the service of the interior life.* If she is speaking she must try to remember that there is One within her to Whom she can speak; if she is listening, let her remember that she can listen to Him Who is nearer to her than anyone else. Briefly, let her realize that, if she likes, *she need never withdraw from this good companionship,* and let her grieve when she has left her Father alone for so long though her need of Him is so sore.
>
> If she can, *let her practice recollection many times daily;* if not, let her do so occasionally. As

she grows accustomed to it, she will feel its benefits, either sooner or later. Once the Lord has granted it to her, she would not exchange it for any treasure.

Nothing, sisters, can be learned without a little trouble, so do, for the love of God, look upon any care which you take about this as well spent. I know that, with God's help, if you practise it for a year, or perhaps for only six months, you will be successful in attaining it. Think what a short time that is for acquiring so great a benefit, for you will be laying a good foundation, so that, if the Lord desires to raise you up to achieve great things, He will find you ready, because you will be close to Himself. (Ibid., ch. 29:1)

This method of prayer is much simpler than the previous form of meditation; it goes directly to its object:

. . . We need no wings to go in search of Him but have only to find a place where we can be alone and look upon Him present within us. Nor need we feel strange in the presence of so kind a Guest; we must talk to Him very humbly, as we should to our father, ask Him for things as we should ask a father, tell Him our troubles, beg Him to put them right, and yet realize that we are not worthy to be called His children. (Ibid., ch. 28:2).

Those who are able to shut themselves up in this way within this little Heaven of the soul, wherein dwells the Maker of Heaven and earth, and who have formed the habit of looking at nothing and staying in no place which will distract these outward senses, may be sure that they are walking on an excellent road, and will come without fail to drink of the water of the fountain, for they will journey a long way in a short time. (Ibid., ch. 28:6)

Control of the senses, which is necessary in order to begin prayer, is more easily accomplished when we form the habit of closing the eyes at prayer, since it is chiefly the sense of sight that will distract us at that time. If the exterior sense through which images enter the soul is disciplined, the interior sense which receives the images, that is, the imagination, will be more easily brought under control and made docile to the service of the soul in prayer. To close the eyes at prayer will gradually help to give us mastery over the senses and direct the soul's gaze inward, since we have nothing exterior to look at.

At first it may cause a good deal of trouble, for the body insists on its rights, not under-standing that if it refuses to admit defeat it is, as it were, cutting off its own head. But if we cul-tivate the habit, make the necessary effort and practise the exercises for several days, the bene-fits will reveal themselves, and when we begin to pray we shall realize that the bees are coming to the hive and entering it to make the honey, and all without any effort of ours. For it is the Lord's will that, in return for the time which their ef-forts have cost them, the soul and the will should be given this power over the senses. They will only have to make a sign to show that they wish to enter into recollection and the senses will obey and allow themselves to be rec-ollected. Later they may come out again, but it is a great thing that they should ever have surren-

dered, for if they come out it is as captives and
slaves and they do none of the harm that they
might have done before. When the will calls
them afresh they respond more quickly, until,
after they have entered the soul many times, the
Lord is pleased that they should remain there al-
together in perfect contemplation. (Ibid., ch.
28:9)

St. Teresa gives us the effects and benefits of
this form of prayer: There is a greater detachment
from outward things, from material and temporal
affairs, although this detachment is still mixed with
many faults. She describes this first step in
detachment thus:

If their recollection is genuine, the fact becomes very evident, for it produces certain effects which I do not know how to explain but
which anyone will recognize who has experience
of them. It is as if the soul were rising from play,
for it sees that worldly things are nothing but
toys; so in due course it rises above them, like a
person entering a strong castle, in order that it
may have nothing more to fear from its enemies.
It withdraws the senses from all outward things
and spurns them so completely that, without its
understanding how, its eyes close and it cannot
see them and the soul's spiritual sight becomes
clear. (Ibid., ch. 28:7)

There are increased desires for God and Divine
Love begins to become enkindled:

. . . The fire of Divine love is the more readily
enkindled in them; for they are so near that fire

that, however little the blaze has been fanned with the understanding, any small spark that flies out at them will cause them to burst into flame. When no hindrance comes to it from outside, the soul remains alone with its God and is thoroughly prepared to become enkindled. (Ibid., ch. 28:9)

Souls who practice this type of recollection "are more secure from many occasions of sin." (Ibid.)

There is greater self-mastery, facility and satisfaction in prayer:

It is a method of prayer which establishes habits that prevent the soul from going astray and the faculties from becoming restless.

It is equivalent to a gradual gaining of the mastery over herself and is not vain labour. To conquer oneself for one's own good is to make use of the senses in the service of the interior life. (ch. 29:7, 9)

This Prayer of Recollection may be entirely mental (as we have noted that it is quiet repose of the soul in the presence of a truth upon which we have just meditated) or it can be partly vocal prayer. In these chapters of the *Way of Perfection* St. Teresa is teaching us how to say the Our Father in this recollected manner.

If one prays in this way, the prayer may be only vocal, but the mind will be recollected much sooner; and this is a prayer which brings with it many blessings. (ch. 28:5)

But whether the prayer be vocal or mental the

soul begins to *enjoy* prayer and *to taste* the first fruits of its labors:

> May the Lord teach this to those of you who do not know it: for my own part I must confess that, until the Lord taught me this method, I never knew what it was to get satisfaction and comfort out of prayer, and it is because I have always gained such great benefits from this custom of interior recollection that I have written about it at such length. (Ibid., ch. 29:8)

Part 2

# THE CALL
# TO
# CONTEMPLATION

## VI.  THE CALL

Meditation and the Prayer of Recollection, with their
various forms, comprise the prayer of beginners in
the spiritual life, or the First Water of prayer, in
which the person labors by his own efforts to drink
of the waters of devotion. St. Teresa says that this
water is not yet *living water*, which God will give to
the soul later on, if it perseveres.

> I should not say that this prayer I have been
> describing, which comes from reasoning with
> the intellect, is living water — I mean so far as
> my understanding of it goes. (*Way of Perfec-
> tion*, ch. 19:6)

But we are called to drink of the living water of
contemplation, a prayer poured into the soul by the
Holy Spirit:

> Remember, the Lord invites us all; and, since
> He is Truth Itself, we cannot doubt Him. If His
> invitation were not a general one, He would not
> have said: "I will give you to drink." He might
> have said: "Come, all of you, for after all you
> will lose nothing by coming; and I will give
> drink to those whom I think fit for it," but as He
> said we were all to come, without making this
> condition, I feel sure that none will fail to receive
> this living water, unless they cannot keep to the
> path. May the Lord, Who promises it, give us
> grace, for His Majesty's own sake, to seek it as it
> must be sought. (Ibid., ch. 19:15)

The Mother of Prayer wants us to learn how to

prepare ourselves to seek this precious gift of perfect prayer as it must be sought, that is, through humility and detachment. She has labored hard to give us detailed instructions on how to prepare.

This call to prayer and contemplation is a call to enter farther into the interior castle of our own souls; there we can explore all those spacious mansions where God dwells.

> In speaking of the soul we must always think of it as spacious, ample and lofty; and this can be done without the least exaggeration, for the soul's capacity is much greater than we can realize, and this Sun, which is in the palace, reaches every part of it. (*Interior Castle*, 1:2:8)
>
> I can find nothing with which to compare the great beauty of a soul and its great capacity. (Ibid., I:1:1)

By its very nature the soul is formed and fitted to know and experience God, and by supernatural virtues such as faith, hope and charity and the Gifts of the Holy Spirit it is actually able to do so, but these gifts are not activated without prayer, so that the person who does not exercise his supernatural endowment will never realize the potential of his own soul, either naturally or supernaturally.

> A short time ago I was told by a very learned man that souls without prayer are like people whose bodies or limbs are paralyzed; they possess feet and hands but they cannot control them. In the same way, there are souls so infirm and so accustomed to busying themselves with outside affairs that nothing can be done for

them, and it seems as though they are incapable of entering within themselves at all . . . *and although by nature they are so richly endowed as to have the power of holding converse with none other than God Himself*, there is nothing that can be done for them. Unless they strive to realize their miserable condition and to remedy it, they will be turned into pillars of salt for not looking within themselves, just as Lot's wife was because she looked back. (Ibid., I:1:6)

Prayer is the door of entry into ourselves and into God, there is no other way:

As far as I can understand, the door of entry into this castle is prayer and meditation . . . I do not say mental prayer rather than vocal, for, if it is prayer at all, it must be accompanied by meditation. If a person does not think Whom he is addressing, and what he is asking for, and who it is that is asking and of Whom he is asking it, I do not consider that he is praying at all even though he be constantly moving his lips. (Ibid., I:1:7)

To persevere in prayer and the kind of life that prayer demands is to progress through the various mansions of the castle until we reach the very center where the King has His throne. *We are all called* to union with Him there because we are all called to holiness, as the Church has reminded us again through the Second Vatican Council:

Therefore in the Church, everyone belonging to the hierarchy, or being cared for by it, is called to holiness, according to the saying of the

Apostle: "For this is the will of God, your sanctification." (*Constitution on the Church*, ch. 5, No. 39)

Thus it is evident to everyone that all the faithful of Christ of whatever rank or status are called to the fullness of the Christian life and to the perfection of charity. (Ibid., No. 40)

Charity is a twofold virtue embracing man in God and God in man simultaneously but it is prayer that gives us the enlightenment. We are Christians in order to serve the cause of love but we cannot until we begin to pray:

> I shall now speak of those who are beginning to be the servants of love — for this, I think, is what we become when we resolve to follow in this way of prayer Him Who so greatly loved us. (St. Teresa, *Life*, ch. 11:1)

We are all called to that *perfect life of love* or to the life of contemplation in which the Holy Spirit is poured into our souls and begins to activate our whole life, but St. Teresa says that few actually prepare themselves for it because they lack generosity with the Lord:

> . . . Few of us prepare ourselves for the Lord to reveal it to us. (*Interior Castle*, 5:1:2)

> . . . It is we alone who are at fault in not at once enjoying so great a dignity. If we attain to the perfect possession of this true love of God, it brings all blessings with it. But so niggardly and so slow are we in giving ourselves wholly to God that we do not prepare ourselves as we should to

receive that precious thing which it is His Majesty's will that we should enjoy only at a great price.

I am quite clear that there is nothing on earth with which so great a blessing can be purchased; but if we did what we could to obtain it, if we cherished no attachment to earthly things and if all our cares and all our intercourse were centered in Heaven, *I believe there is no doubt that this blessing would be given us very speedily, provided we prepared ourselves for it thoroughly and quickly, as did some of the saints.* But we think we are giving God everything, whereas what we are really offering Him is the revenue or the fruits of our land while keeping the stock and the right of ownership of it in our own hands. We have made a resolve to be poor, and that is a resolution of great merit; but we often begin to plan and strive again so that we may have no lack, not only of necessaries, but even of superfluities; we try to make friends who will give us these, lest we should lack anything; and we take greater pains, and perhaps even run greater risks, than we did before, when we had possessions of our own. Presumably, again, when we became nuns, or previously, when we began to lead spiritual lives and to follow after perfection, we abandoned all thought of our own importance; and yet hardly is our self-importance wounded than we quite forget that we have surrendered it to God and we try to seize it again, and wrest it, as they say, out of His very hands, although we had apparently made Him Lord of our will. And the same happens with everything else. (*Life,* ch. 11:1, 2)

It is only with great reluctance that we

relinquish our own excessive love of ourselves. A magnanimous love for God is absolutely necessary or we will never be able to do it at all.

## VII. HOW DO WE PREPARE OURSELVES FOR THE LIFE OF PRAYER?

### A. To Realize the Great Dignity and Capacity of Our Souls and to Take Care of Them

What we must do first of all is to realize the great dignity and capacity of our souls and take care of them:

> The soul is as capable of enjoying Him as is the crystal of reflecting the sun. (*Interior Castle*, I:2:1)

and:

> ... The utmost we have to do at first is *to take care of our soul* and to remember that in the entire world there is only God and the soul; and this is a thing which it is very profitable to remember. (*Life*, ch. 13:9)

> ... The soul of the righteous man is nothing but a paradise, in which, as God tells us, He takes His delight. (*Interior Castle*, I:1:1)

Meditation on this fundamental truth will open our souls in confidence and expand our always too narrow horizons, so that we will thirst for much, and thus hoping much, we will be able to receive much.

Next, St. Teresa counsels us that prayer must

bring us into conformity with the will of God, for that is the beginning and the end of prayer:

> All that the beginner in prayer has to do — and you must not forget this, for it is very important — *is to labour and be resolute and prepare himself with all possible diligence to bring his will into conformity with the will of God.* As I shall say later, you may be quite sure that this comprises the very greatest perfection which can be attained on the spiritual road. The more perfectly a person practises it, the more he will receive the Lord and the greater the progress he will make on this road. . . . (Ibid., II:1:9)

## B. To Strive for Perfect Conformity with the Will of God

Bringing our wills into conformity with the will of God would be an easy thing for us if there were no sin and self-will. We would not need courage and resolutions but only a simple act of agreement and acquiescence. Our present state of affairs, however, requires great resolution, determination and courage to resist the alluring illusions that pull us away from truth.

For this reason our meditations must be practical, that is, they must have a real relation to our daily lives by helping to bring us into Christ's life and Christ into ours. They must often be aimed at particular virtues that we personally need and vices that require correction. Our meditations on the virtues of Christ and His Mother must be joined to examination of ourselves and insight on how these virtues can be put into daily practice. That takes courage and determination, because it means facing ourselves, and this facing ourselves in truth is the work which must be done before we can come into union with the will of God.

• Courage and Resolution in Bearing Trials

Conformity with the will of God also means courage and resolution in persevering through the inevitable trials that come during prayer itself and often because of it. In her *Life*, St. Teresa tells us what we are to do when these periods of dryness and helplessness come upon us and it seems that we can do nothing during our prayer time.

> What, then, will he do here who finds that for many days he experiences nothing but aridity, dislike, distaste and so little desire to go and draw water that he would give it up entirely if he did not remember that he is pleasing and serving the Lord of the garden; if he were not anxious that all his service should not be lost, to say nothing of the gain which he hopes for from the great labour of lowering the bucket so often into the well and drawing it up without water? It will often happen that, even for that purpose, he is unable to move his arms — unable, that is, to think a single good thought, for working with the understanding is of course the same as drawing water out of the well. What, then, as I say, will the gardener do here? He will be glad and take heart and consider it the greatest of favour to work in the garden of so great an Emperor; and, as he knows that he is pleasing Him by so working (and his purpose must be to please, not

himself, but Him), let him render Him great praise for having placed such confidence in him, when He has seen that, without receiving any recompense, he is taking such great care of that which He had entrusted to him; let him help Him to bear the Cross and consider how He lived with it all His life long; let him not wish to have his kingdom on earth or ever cease from prayer; and so let him resolve, even if this aridity should persist his whole life long, never to let Christ fall beneath the Cross. The time will come when he shall receive his whole reward at once. Let him have no fear that his labour will be lost. He is serving a good Master, Whose eyes are upon him. Let him pay no heed to evil thoughts, remembering how the devil put such thoughts into the mind of Saint Jerome in the desert. (ch. 11:10)

Such trials come upon us in order to purify our service of God and to help us bend our wills to His, so that when it seems we cannot pray, the acceptance of that very condition becomes our prayer. There is always something for the soul to do in prayer. God never leaves it completely bound and unable to move. When we can think nothing and the heart is cold as stone, we can offer Him acts of acceptance. We can be glad we are having no satisfaction and offer Him the pleasure and glory of all the delights of Heaven while we pay the price. We can give Him the joy of our abandonment in darkness and bitter discomfort; we can ratify all His just judgments in giving us the nothing that our nothingness deserves. We can glory in our infirmities and even rejoice that we are and have nothing, and experience nothing that could give us any comfort and satisfaction, and in so doing, in darkness and unknown to ourselves, we give Him much glory and expand immensely in faith, hope and pure love, refined a thousand times in aridity and affliction. There is an incident in the life of Sister Josefa Menendez (Society of the Sacred Heart) R.S.C.J., (1890-1923) that is enlightening and encouraging. During a period of intense temptation, aridity and affliction in which she could not pray, she says:

> In the midst of this storm I was able to repeat only these words: "Jesus, Jesus, forsake me not." Awful thoughts had taken possession of my mind and I implored Our Lady to stop me in time if I were not in a fit state to go to Holy Communion. . . . My time of prayer was spent in this way. Then Mass; I went to Holy Communion, but could only call on Jesus to help me, and say over and over again: "I believe that Thou art in the depths of my soul, O my God — indeed I believe it." Suddenly I heard His answering voice: "I am there."
>
> "When I leave you so cold," He said, "I am using your warmth to give heat to other souls. When I leave you a prey to anguish, your suffering wards off divine justice when it is about to strike sinners. When it seems to you as if you did not love Me and yet you tell Me unceasingly that you do, then you console My Heart most. That is what I want: that you should be ready to comfort My Heart every time I need you." (*The Way of Divine Love*, p. 56)

This incident is a modern and living ratification of St. Teresa's words. From the Lord's own mouth we learn that our prayer is to comfort Him and help

Him bear the Cross, to win grace for souls by reparation and vicarious suffering in the endurance of our own necessary purifications. Our hearts can be filled with praise and gratitude to think that even the sufferings we must undergo for our own failings and sins, that is, our own purgations of culpable sin, can be and are used by Him for the salvation of others. Our faith and trust can feed for hours on this knowledge, even when it does not initiate other reflections to occupy our minds or ignite any spark to enflame our hearts. In darkness and aridity, the soul is growing, becoming stronger and being nourished by His very secret and hidden presence. To answer St. Teresa's question then: "What should the soul do, and where shall it go in such times of trial?" . . . it should fly to His Heart and rest there in trust and abandonment, in dark faith:

> When a soul is burnt up with desire to love, nothing is a burden to her, but if she feels cold and spiritless everything becomes hard and difficult — Let her then come to My Heart and revive her courage . . . Let her offer Me her dejection, and unite it to My fervour; then she may rest content, for her day will be of incomparable value to souls. All human miseries are known to My Heart, and My compassion for them is great.
>
> But I desire souls to unite themselves to Me not only in a general way. I long for this union to be constant and intimate as it is between friends who live together; for even if they are not talking all the time, at least they look at each other, and their mutual affectionate little kindnesses are the fruit of their love.

When a soul is in peace and consolation, doubtless it is easier for her to think of Me, but if she is in the throes of desolation and anguish, she need not fear. I am content with a glance. I understand, and this mere look will draw down on her special proofs of My tenderness.

I ardently desire My chosen souls to fix their eyes on Me, and never turn them away.... (Ibid., pp. 237-8)

Thus we see that we can always give glory to Him in whatever state of prayer, or lack of prayer, we find ourselves. The faith in darkness and the trust in His love become our prayer. The soul learns to converse with God more humbly and to seek Him more secretly in dark faith, which St. John of the Cross says we must learn to do in order to advance to the state where we live only to give God glory.

... Seek Him in faith and love, without desire for the satisfaction, taste, or understanding of any other thing than what you ought to know. Faith and love are like the blind man's guides. They will lead you along a path unknown to you, to the place where God is hidden.

You do very well, O soul, to seek Him ever as one hidden, for you exalt God immensely and approach very near Him when you consider Him higher and deeper than anything you can reach. Hence, pay no attention, neither partially nor entirely, to anything which your faculties can grasp. *I mean that you should never desire satisfaction in what you understand about God*, but in what you do not understand about Him. Never stop with loving and delighting in your understanding and experience of God, but love and delight in what is neither understandable nor perceptible of Him. Such is the way, as we said, of seeking Him in faith. However surely it may seem that you find, experience, and understand God, you must, because He is inaccessible and concealed, always regard Him as hidden, and serve Him Who is hidden in a secret way. Do not be like the many foolish ones who, in their lowly understanding of God, think that when they do not understand, taste, or experience Him, He is far away and utterly concealed. The contrary belief would be truer. The less distinct is their understanding of Him, the closer they approach Him, since in the words of the prophet David, "He made darkness His hiding place." (Psalms 17:12) Thus in drawing near Him, you will experience darkness because of the weakness of your eye.

You do well, then, at all times, in both adversity and prosperity, whether spiritual or temporal, to consider God as hidden. . . . (*Spiritual Canticle*, st. 1:11-12)

We can come to enjoy our own little meditations so much that we become attached to them. So, to loosen our hold on ourselves and our own thoughts about God, however good they may be and however much they may have helped us, God Himself takes them from us through the trials of aridity and darkness, helplessness and affliction during prayer. He seems to block up all communication with Him so that we will learn by experience the lesson we read from St. John: even though we need to think about God and experience God, what we *think about* Him and *experience* of Him *is not God Himself* and no sure sign of His presence. His presence is not consolation, or ability to think of Him, or delight in Him. *It is essentially the degree to which His power and grace are actually moving and activating our whole lives through faith, hope and charity.*

Sometimes when we feel that He is farthest from us He is actually closer to us through the secret and hidden action of His grace which makes us seek Him in painful and longing affliction. If He were not present to us as the object of our love and desire we would not miss Him or feel His absence or even desire to seek the consolation of His presence in affectionate love again. His very absence is a presence drawing us onward to expand in faith. The *Imitation* confirms this by giving us this consoling passage for our instruction:

> Believe in Me and trust in My mercy. When you think I am far from you, I am often nearest to you. When you judge that almost all is lost, then oftentimes it is that you are in the way of gaining the greatest merit.
>
> All is not lost when anything falls out otherwise than you would have it. You must not judge according to your present feeling, nor give yourself up in such manner to any trouble, whencesoever it comes, nor take it so as if all hope were gone of being delivered out of it.
>
> Think not yourself wholly forsaken, although for a time I have sent you some tribulation, or withdrawn from you the comfort which you desire; for this is the way to the kingdom of heaven.
>
> And without doubt it is more expedient for you, and for the rest of My servants, that you be

exercised by adversities than that you should have all things according to your inclination.

I know your secret thoughts; I know that it is very expedient for your soul that you should sometimes be left without consolation, lest you should be puffed up with much success and should take a complacence in yourself, imagining yourself to be what you are not.

What I have given I can justly take away and restore it again when I please. When I give it, it is still Mine; when I take it away again I take not anything that is yours; for every good gift and every perfect gift is Mine. (James 1:17).

If I send you affliction or any adversity, repine not, neither let your heart be cast down. I can quickly raise you up again and turn all your burden into joy. Nevertheless, I am just and greatly to be praised when I deal thus with you. If you think rightly and consider things in truth you ought never to be so much dejected and troubled for any adversity, but rather to rejoice and give thanks. Yea, even to account this as a special subject of joy, that afflicting you with sorrows I spare you not. (Job 6:10)

As My Father has loved Me I also have loved you, said I to My beloved disciples (John 15:9), whom certainly I did not send to temporal joys, but to great conflicts; not to honors, but to contempt; not to idleness but to labors; not to rest, but to "bring forth much fruit in patience" (Luke 8:15). Remember these words, O my son. (Book III, ch. 30:3-6)

We must be tested before we are admitted to His intimacy in that infusion of the Holy Spirit called contemplation, in fact, the very passage through the desert of darkness and aridity is the gateway to contemplation. Here in the First water, St. Teresa wants the beginner to understand that we must work hard but peacefully at our meditations because, as she says:

> . . . Recollection cannot be begun by making strenuous efforts, but must come gently, after which you will be able to practise it for longer periods at a time. (*Interior Castle*, II:2:11)

But we must also realize that meditation is not the end and goal of our prayer life, it is a means and a stepping-stone to contemplative prayer which can only be reached through the courageous and faithful endurance of many trials and testings in prayer. "Through many tribulations we enter into the kingdom of God." (Acts 14:21) But patience will gradually bring forth fruit:

> These trials bring their own reward. I endured them for many years; and, when I was able to draw but one drop of water from this blessed well, I used to think that God was granting me a favour. I know how grievous such trials are and I think they need more courage than do many others in the world. But it has become clear to me that, even in this life, God does not fail to recompense them highly; for it is quite certain that a single one of those hours in which the Lord has granted me to taste of Himself has seemed to me later a recompense for all the afflictions which I endured over a long period while keeping up the practise of prayer. I believe myself that often in the early stages, and again

later, it is the Lord's will to give us these tortures, and many other temptations which present themselves, in order to test His lovers and discover if they can drink of the chalice and help Him to bear the Cross before He trusts them with His treasures. I believe it is for our good that His Majesty is pleased to lead us in this way so that we may have a clear understanding of our worthlessness; for the favours which come later are of such great dignity that before He grants us them He wishes us to know by experience how miserable we are, lest what happened to Lucifer happen to us also. (*Life*, ch. 11:11)

The soul then must not strive for consolations but bear its burden humbly and hope that in its weakness and poverty it may be pleasing to God, and though it may often feel like shirking the effort to make itself pray, it must always do so, because sooner or later the water will come, as St. Teresa says from her own experience:

I used to feel so depressed that I had to summon up all my courage to make myself pray at all . . . In the end, the Lord would come to my help. Afterwards, when I had forced myself to pray, I would find that I had more tranquillity and happiness than at certain other times when I had prayed because I had wanted to. (*Life*, ch. 8:7)

When we cannot pray and our thoughts are wandering everywhere at rapid pace, we can often be helped by slow reflective reading, sentence by sentence, but we must be careful not to turn our time of prayer into spiritual reading and then, over a period of time, get used to the habit, so that we never really learn to pray in aridity and darkness.

Cultivation of this habit of cheerfully offering to the Lord the sacrifice of our helplessness and affliction in prayer is one of the chief means of swiftly arriving at true freedom of spirit in the spiritual life and a pure love for Him.

> If a person would gain spiritual freedom and not be continually troubled, let him begin by not being afraid of the Cross and he will find that the Lord will help him to bear it; he will then advance happily and find profit in everything. It is now clear that, if no water is coming from the well, we ourselves can put none into it. But of course we must not be careless: water must always be drawn when there is any there, for at such a time God's will is that we should use it so that He may multiply our virtues. (*Life*, ch. 11:17)

• Helpful Means of Perseverance

• To transform our aridities, afflictions, suffering, trials, humiliations, poverty and helplessness into joy is one of the most powerful and rapid means of transformation of soul, because it is going against the grain of our natural desires for pleasure and satisfaction in everything and at all times. To rejoice when we are miserable; to rejoice that we have no consolation so that He can have it all; to rejoice that we are poor and really feeling our poverty of soul; to rejoice that we are painfully conscious that we can do nothing without His grace;

114

to rejoice when we are cold, distracted, weak and our soul feels sick and sore inside of us, though we are not aware of any disloyalty to God, or perhaps *even* when *we know that we are* suffering the results of little acts of ungenerosity and carelessness; to rejoice *then* is to love God truly and at our expense. It is in those very moments when we have our finest hour, our moment of glory wherein we are perhaps more courageous than if we were capable of heroic deeds that would attract the admiration of multitudes. "Power is made perfect in infirmity" (2 Corinthians 12:9), and soon our infirmity will become the very foundation on which the Lord will build the Castle of prayer.

> It must be carefully noted — and I say this because I know it by experience — that the soul which begins to walk resolutely in this way of mental prayer and can persuade itself to set little store by consolations and tenderness in devotion, and neither to be elated when the Lord gives them nor disconsolate when He withholds them, has already travelled a great part of its journey. However often it may stumble, it need not fear a relapse, for its building has been begun on a firm foundation. Yes, love for God does not consist in shedding tears, in enjoying those consolations and that tenderness which for the most part we desire and in which we find comfort, but in serving Him with righteousness, fortitude of soul and humility. The other seems to me to be receiving rather than giving anything. (St. Teresa, *Life*, ch. 11:13)

• To be able to love Him purely without looking for our immediate payment in the form of constant consolations is to live the life of *faith*, so glorious and so meritorious and so pleasing to God. It is when we give Him all the joy without having any of it ourselves, that we give Him the greatest proof of love. The deepest joy we have on earth is that of being deprived of the experience of it for the love of Jesus. That is a joy that few people ever taste because their love is too weak.

• It has already been said that prayer is an homage of the whole person, an activity of the soul, the mind and the will and not a passing emotion. There are some who yield to discouragement when they are bored in prayer, abandon prayer and turn away from Christ to more interesting aspects of the apostolate or even useless pastimes, because they do not feel His Presence and are without consolation. These are not His true lovers and seek themselves, not Christ. If they sought Him alone, they would sooner or later taste of His sweetness, His infused strength and rest in prayer, that is, they would come at last to experience true contemplation. In hours of trial and suffering, we must imitate Him in the Agony of the Garden, *prolonging prayer precisely because we need it most then*, and if we keep on crying for help, eventually it will come. When we do not feel like it, is exactly when we need prayer because, when we do not feel like it, is the very moment we will be most susceptible to temptation, since our souls are less securely guarded by the close presence of God. We must pray to enter more deeply and consciously into that presence to secure ourselves from dangers; we must pray for patience and persistence.

• St. Teresa tells us *not to be afflicted* or to give

up prayer when we cannot manage our thoughts. We may then be growing much in pure love, although we are not aware of it. We are not to think that prayer consists in thought, but in love proved in trial:

> When the understanding ceases to work, they cannot bear it, though perhaps even then the will is increasing in power, and putting on new strength, without their knowing it. We must realize that the Lord pays no heed to these things: to us they may look like faults, but they are not so. His Majesty knows our wretchedness and the weakness of our nature better than we ourselves and He knows that all the time these souls are longing to think of Him and to love Him. It is this determination that He desires in us.
>
> ... And so it is well that prayer should not always be given up when the mind is greatly distracted and disturbed, nor the soul tormented by being made to do what is not in its power.
>
> I repeat my advice, then (and it matters not how often I say this, for it is of great importance), that *one must never be depressed or afflicted because of aridities or un/est or distraction of the mind. (Life*, ch. 11:15-17)

There is also a very consoling instruction which the Lord one day gave to St. Gertrude on this difficulty of directing our thoughts to God. She received this answer to her question:

> ... When man raises his mind to heaven by meditation or reflection, he presents, as it were, before the throne of God's glory a bright and shining mirror, in which the Lord beholds His

own image with pleasure, because He is the Author and Dispenser of all good. And the more difficulty any one finds in this elevation of soul, the more perfect and agreeable this mirror appears before the Most Holy Trinity and the saints, and it will remain for the eternal glory of God and the good of this soul. (*Life and Revelations of St. Gertrude*, Newman, 1949, p. 200)

It is our effort He seeks not our success.

    • We need a prudent balance in life.

In such times of trial and helplessness one may and, in fact, should sometimes change occupation in order to refresh oneself. To do something else to relieve and recreate ourselves is not abandoning prayer but fortifying ourselves for another attempt. Human nature often needs only a little recreation in order to return to prayer invigorated. St. Teresa gives us this wise counsel:

> There are other things which can be done — exterior acts, such as reading or works of charity — though sometimes the soul will be unable to do even these. At such times the soul must render the body a service for the love of God, so that on many other occasions the body may render services to the soul. Engage in some spiritual recreation, such as conversation (so long as it is really spiritual), or a country walk . . . Sweet is His yoke, and it is essential that we should not drag the soul along with us, so to say, but lead it gently, so that it may make the greater progress. (*Life*, ch. 11:16)

In the early stages, then, one should strive to feel happy and free. There are some people who think that devotion will slip away from them if they relax a little. It is well to have misgivings about oneself and not to allow self-confidence to lead one into occasions which habitually involve offenses against God . . . Yet there are many circumstances in which, as I have said, it is permissible for us to take some recreation, in order that we may be the stronger when we return to prayer. In everything we need discretion. (Ibid., ch. 13:1)

St. Teresa knew that the constant application of our minds to prayer and recollection must be balanced and tempered by light-hearted and wholesome recreation which would not only relax the body but refresh the soul.

• Whatever happens *we must never give up prayer:*

Never give up your hours of prayer: you do not know when the Bridegroom will summon you, and you might share the fate of the foolish virgins. (*Way of Perfection*, ch. 18:4)

If he does not give up prayer, let him be assured of this . . . prayer will bring him to the haven of light. (*Letters* of St. Teresa, No. 19:7)

St. Teresa assures us that even the so-called obstacles to prayer such as aridity, distraction, impotence to think anything good, burdens of worries and anxieties can even be used as the subject of our prayer and can help prayer.

. . . Despite illness, or other hindrances, we can still engage in true prayer, when there is love

119

in the soul, by offering up that very impediment, remembering Him for Whom we suffer it and being resigned to it and to a thousand other things which may happen to us. It is here that love comes in: for we are not necessarily praying when we are alone, nor need we refrain from praying when we are not.

With a little care, great blessings can be acquired at times when the Lord deprives us of our hours of prayer by sending us trials; and this I had myself found to be the case when my conscience had been good. (*Life*, ch. 11:12-13)

Trials, struggle, resolution, courage and love, all serve to bring our wills into union with the holy will of God and prepare us to drink of the fountain of living water which is contemplation.

## C. Mortification Specifically Adapted to Prayer

In addition to these fundamental requirements in preparing our souls for contemplative prayer, that is, a deep realization of the dignity and capacity of our souls and constancy in trial fortified by love of Jesus, we need that specific mortification which is aimed directly at prayer: namely, the discipline of our thought, our curiosity, our imaginings and our memories. Dissipation and negligence in regulating our interior life has very serious consequences. Certainly if our minds are taken up with the happenings of the day or our souls agitated by useless affections, jealousy, wounded self-love, the memory of real or imagined wrongs and slights that have come to us that day, or by rash judgments and excessive zeal for the correction of other people's faults which bother us, we will not be able to converse with the Lord. All these interior problems are the result of inordinate affection and attachment to self, and if pure love of God does not replace them the soul will never be able to rise above these petty things to rest in God in distress as well as in consolation. This carelessness and lack of silence in the interior is the reason why the Gifts of the Holy Spirit are almost without effect in us. We are able to grow and expand in the Christ-life, by His virtues and Gifts, but often we are not growing. A true spirit of prayer is impossible without true interior austerity. Unmortified passion and desire hinder the secret impulses of the Holy Spirit and we cannot afford to lose even one of the Lord's precious words to the soul.

> Blessed is that soul which hears the Lord speaking within her (Proverbs 8:34), and from His mouth receives the word of comfort.
> Blessed ears which receive the accents of the divine whisper and take no notice of the whispers of the world.
> Blessed ears indeed, which hearken to truth itself teaching within and not to the voice which sounds without.
> Blessed eyes which are shut to outward things and attentive to the interior.
> Blessed they who penetrate into the internal things and endeavor to prepare themselves more and more by daily exercises to the attainment of heavenly secrets.
> Blessed they who seek to be wholly intent on God and who rid themselves of every worldly impediment.

Mind these things, O my soul, and shut the doors of your sensuality, that you may hear what the Lord your God speaks within you. (*Imitation*, Bk. III, ch. 1:1)

These are the beatitudes of the interior life and the reward of those who hear His Word and keep it. They will draw closer to the Lord in the union of contemplation.

## D. Prudence in Attending to Ourselves and God

One more very practical caution for advancement in the prayer life is given us by St. Teresa to beginners who, from a little success in prayer, become overly zealous and wish to correct everyone else's defects and be considered very spiritual themselves.

> There is another temptation which is very common — namely to desire that every one should be extremely spiritual when one is beginning to find what tranquillity and what profit, spirituality brings. It is not wrong to desire this but it may not be right to try to bring it about unless we do so with such discretion and dissimulation that we give no impression of wanting to teach others. For if a person is to do any good in this respect he must be very strong in the virtues so as not to put temptation in others' way. . . .
> Another temptation comes from the distress caused by the sins and failings which we see in others, for we all have a zeal for virtue and so we must learn to understand ourselves and walk

warily. The devil tells us that this distress arises solely from our desire that God should not be offended and from our concern for His honour and then we immediately try to set matters right. This makes us so excited that it prevents us from praying, and the greatest harm of all is that we think this to be a virtue, and a sign of perfection and of great zeal for God. I am not referring to the distress caused by public offences in a religious congregation, if they become habitual, or of wrongs done to the Church, such as heresies, through which, as we see, so many souls are lost; for distress caused by these is right, and, being right, causes us no excitement. Safety, then, for the soul that practises prayer will consist in its *ceasing to be anxious about anything and anybody, and in its watching itself and pleasing God.* This is most important. If I were to describe the mistakes I have seen people make because they trusted in their good intentions . . .! (*Life*, ch. 13:8, 10)

If we mind our own business and attend to God we will avoid much harm and many distractions in our journey to Him. True zeal is peaceful, it never disturbs or disquiets the soul. Until we are strong enough in virtue to exercise it properly we must attend to the cultivation of our own garden.

. . . There is another great disadvantage in yielding to this temptation: namely, the harm caused to our own soul; for the utmost we have to do at first is to take care of our soul and to remember that in the entire world there is only God and the soul; and this is a thing which it is very profitable to remember. (*Life*, ch. 13:9)

St. Teresa tells us in Chapters 7 and 8 of her *Life* that it was to this first water of prayer that the conversion of her life must be attributed. Through prayer she was able to amend the negligent spiritual life she had been living for almost eighteen years. Without prayer there will be no amendment:

> For it is the means by which we may amend our lives again, and without it amendment will be very much harder. So let him not be tempted by the devil, as I was, to give it up for reasons of humility, but let him believe that the words cannot fail of Him Who says that, if we truly repent and determine not to offend Him, He will resume His former friendship with us and grant us the favours which He granted aforetime, and sometimes many more, if our repentance merits it. And anyone who has not begun to pray, I beg, for love of the Lord, not to miss so great a blessing. There is no place here for fear, but only for desire. For, even if a person fails to make progress, or to strive after perfection, so that he may merit the consolations and favours given to the perfect by God, *yet he will gradually gain a knowledge of the road to Heaven. (Life*, ch. 8:5)

## VIII.   PRAYER: FRIENDSHIP WITH GOD

Friendship dies when communication ceases and we cannot allow that to happen when our only true friend is the Lord, our Savior and Father and Bridegroom:

For when you never have intercourse with a person he soon becomes a stranger to you, and you forget how to talk to him; and before long, even if he is a kinsman, you feel as if you do not know him, for both kinship and friendship lose their influence when communication ceases." (*Way of Perfection*, ch. 26:9)

## A. God's Ways of Dealing with the Soul in Prayer

Our whole life must be given over to the cultivation of this friendship and to do so we must know more about God's ways of dealing with the soul in prayer. He enlightens, he comforts and consoles, He corrects and rebukes our faults, He chastises and He heals. He is in every way a loving father most solicitous that we become neither overly elated and complacent when He consoles us nor cast down and dejected when He scolds us. For as the *Imitation* says, He visits the soul in two ways:

> I am accustomed to visit My elect in two ways: that is, by trial and by comfort and I read them daily two lessons, one to rebuke their vices, the other to exhort them to the increase of virtues. (Bk. III, ch. 3:5)

Usually He gives us a taste of His sweetness and then He humbles us by exposing a fault. Like a father He lifts the child up to His cheek and then He points out a failing to be corrected. We may have had an hour of successful prayer, according to our estimation, and then go off to some duty wherein we come face to face with a great personal defect. Has

He left us? No, this very light revealing the dark side of our character is a sign of His presence, it is an *effect* of that prayer wherein we thought we had a hold on Him. Now in humiliation and the confusion of our minds we come to recognize Him in His correcting action. He lays bare the wounds of our character and causes the blood of contrition to flow, then He takes us back up in His arms and heals the sore spot with a kiss.

Sometimes He hides behind authority to correct us, or uses authority to heal what He will not heal in prayer by the gift of His consoling presence. He may leave the soul in dryness and affliction for a long time expecting it to find light, strength and peace only from contact and humble openness of soul with the Church, with authority, that is, through the sacramental life. His action permeates everywhere and He will never leave us alone if we will let Him act. Thus gradually He weaves and interweaves prayer into our whole life and every part of it. Every instant is touched with prayer when we are open to His saving action. Each day there are new lights, new inspirations, new enkindlings in love and the person changes, step by step, into a deeper relationship with Him. Little by little the prayer also changes because the life is changing, for every change in prayer, every advance in prayer, is a change in the entire life. Our whole being is becoming transformed, not just our manner of praying.

Holiness consists in the faithful cooperation of the soul in the secret designs of God. It is begun, grows and is perfected in the soul unperceived and in the hidden depths, while we observe only the exteriors of the apparent vicissitudes of life. Our whole work consists in training ourselves to recognize the workings of God in the present moment and these moments are made fruitful only through the cooperation with His will, often in blind and uncomprehending faith.

## B.  Our Dispositions Toward Him: Littleness

Humility is the heart and foundation of any communion with God as St. Teresa tells us in her *Life:*

> What I have learned is this: that *the entire foundation of prayer must be established in humility,* and that, the more a soul abases itself in prayer, the higher God raises it. I do not remember that He has ever granted me any of the outstanding favours of which I shall speak later save when I have been consumed with same by realizing my own wickedness; and His Majesty has even managed to help me to know myself by revealing to me things which I myself could not have imagined. (ch. 22:11)

He who humbles himself will be exalted. This is the mystery of God's ways with men and the mystery of His relationship with us in prayer.

> As, the foundation of the entire edifice is humility, the nearer we come to God, the greater must be the progress which we make in this virtue: otherwise, we lose everything. (*Life*, ch. 12:4)

127

The humble soul always receives a reward in many secret little ways by which the Lord reveals Himself. Even in times of aridity and darkness He has His inimitable means of letting us know He is there, of sending us little testimonies of His love, of His constant care and solicitous attention, through the smile or kindness of others, through the daily gift of simple natural benefits and pleasures, and through the continual renewal of His total gift of Himself in the Mass and the Eucharist. The humble soul is never left alone nor ever made to wait too long for the visit of God in His mercy, as St. John of the Cross says:

> It is noteworthy that God is very ready to comfort and satisfy the soul in her needs and afflictions when she neither has nor desires consolation and satisfaction outside of Him. The soul possessing nothing that might withhold her from God cannot remain long without a visit from the Beloved. (*Spiritual Canticle*, st. 10:6)

The quickest way to reach a deep union with God in prayer is the way of the "little ones" who live totally dependent on God, seeing His hand and blessing It in everything that happens to them, both bitter and sweet. To abandon oneself entirely to Him is the perfection of the prayer life. He gives His peace to those who have made themselves nothing in their own eyes; they are masters over His Heart. Like the tiny point of a needle which can penetrate the densest material, an humble soul can pierce the Heart of God and cause the flow of Divine grace to pour out over the ills of the world of souls.

128

The humility which lives dependent on Him, trusting in His grace and mercy, is all-powerful and can obtain what great feats of penance, austerity, long vigils, and heroic acts cannot without this spirit of humble and obedient trust. His intimates are the humble and poor in spirit to whom He gives His joy, His peace and His wisdom, unknown to the worldly-wise and prudent. To these, the "little ones," He gives everything and no door is closed to them. They can penetrate into the innermost mansions where the King dwells. The whole castle and all of its treasures belong to them.

The last and final Mansions, the seventh one, is the adobe of the humble and their rightful inheritance, because the door is so small that they alone can enter there. Straight is the way to the deepest union with God and narrow the gate, and only humility will find it. So that if we would live this life with Him we must live it as He would have it lived. We must be to Him as His tiny child and then we will understand His ways of dealing with us in the life of prayer. We will know how to receive His communications and how to respond. There is only one thing that counts in His eyes, the trustful love and complete abandonment of a little soul, so that to advance in the life of prayer we must forget everything else and strive with all our might to acquire this pearl of the greatest price: humility of Christ. Then we will have won the King Himself and His whole Kingdom.

# IX.  THE APOSTOLATE OF PRAYER

## A.  Prayer Is Service

We have to be absolutely convinced that prayer is a
very particular means of service to the Church and
the world, which is so presently concerned about
service. A life of prayer is the service Jesus rendered
to the world on Calvary. Nailed to all the world's
means of human satisfaction and fulfillment, He
served men by enduring their chastisement, their ills
and results of their sins, and under this inhuman
burden of unjust and unmerited suffering He won
their redemption by obtaining their pardon through
prayer. To do what He did, to really live the life of
prayer, one must advance through all the stages of
death to sin and reconstruction of the soul, until one
is situated in the whole Christ, transformed into
Him. One passes through Calvary to the
resurrection. Anyone who has done that has done a
real service to humanity, whether humanity
recognizes its benefit or not.

The one who prays will, sooner or later, face all
the struggles, temptations and solicitations to sin and
evil that have plagued the soul of man from the
beginning. All alone in the solitude of our little
interior castles we must battle for every virtue,
against every contrary force and know from
experience the face-to-face struggle with Satan for
possession of the soul. Through the denial of our
desires we can, for example, feed the starving
millions, because the Savior, through the economy

130

of redemption and the mystery of reparation and vicarious suffering, uses little acts of sacrifice to bring grace to others in need. Each denial of even a spoonful of sweetness which we might crave, is multiplied by Him as He multiplied the loaves and fishes to feed the multitude. Each day that we give Him our widow's mite of little acts repeated over and over, He dispenses the vast treasures and immense riches of His kingdom to the needy. Through our Christian lives of sacrifice we add to the Church's storerooms, and through our prayer we join in the distribution. We are millionaires with grace and in the spiritual realm, we are able to satisfy all our longings to relieve the misery of the miserable.

Prayer coupled with self-denial is our outlet for the desires of our heart to do endless good. As we have said, we can practice all the works of mercy in a spiritual way and through the most efficacious means. Our prayer feeds the hungry and inspires the well-fed to give; it clothes the naked, gives drink to the thirsty. It visits the sick, and comforts the dying, consoles the depressed, gives light to the blind, finds employment for the poor, instructs the ignorant, and counsels the doubtful. To check an unnecessary word and offer it to the Lord is to stop a flow of sinful or blasphemous words somewhere else in the world. To conquer Satan in our own hearts and minds, even by the stoppage of a single useless, critical or unkind thought, is to lessen his power everywhere. Satan is extremely afraid of the soul that prays because such a person paralyzes his work. He will do all he can to keep anyone from an hour or even a minute of recollected and concentrated prayer.

## B. The Power Of This Service

We often allow ourselves to grow slack and listless in prayer because we have not let these truths sink deeply enough into our minds. The more we come to know God and the power of prayer with Him, and 1 to know our own needs and thus the needs of men, the more we will value prayer. We will learn to pray better by believing intensely in its efficacy. Prayer is a far stronger instrument than preaching or writing or exhorting, though all of these are necessary and not to be neglected; but we can do little by word or writing if prayer is lacking or spiritless. When we believe, prayer is omnipotent:

> I tell you therefore: everything you ask and pray for, believe that you have it already, and it will be yours. (Mark 11:24)

God has promised everything to prayer. The life of any saint is a marvelous contest between God and the soul struggling for grace and salvation. The soul comes to experience its weakness prevailing with His greatness. It comes to taste the power of the little one, who like the smallest child in the family can do nothing, yet it receives all simply because of its omnipotent weakness. What father is not completely conquered by the utter helplessness of his smallest child? So God is conquered and weak against the assaults of even the least prayer of the soul who trusts totally to Him, and belongs totally to Him.

> The soul that belongs to Me no longer belongs to anyone else, but like Me and with Me

she belongs to the human race. You must pray for all. (*Spiritual Legacy of Sister Mary of the Trinity*, Newman, Westminster, Md., 1954)

From the very beginning of our attempt at prayer we must be convinced of the splendor of a life of prayer and its efficacy in the apostolate of perpetuating the praise, adoration, thanksgiving, and supplication of all mankind, in the person of every man, and in behalf of each individual.

> The time that you have spent in praying and loving has been the most useful time of your life; then you have obeyed your vocation — all that is done apart from Me, apart from love, is wasted. (Ibid., No. 227)

## X.  OUR MOTHER MARY AND HER PLACE IN OUR COMMUNION WITH GOD

Devotion and close association with our Most Blessed Mother is the most efficacious means of growing in the prayer-life and the transformation into Jesus, because where Mary is there is Jesus. She always leads to Him. If we love Mary, she will make us love Jesus. She is the fullness of grace shared with us in prayer and is therefore at the very heart of our Christian vocation. Mary teaches us how to listen to Jesus and receive the least motion of His Divine impulses. She will show us how to hear the Word of God and keep it; how to root out all our attachments and hindrances to grace. She is the ocean of grace filled by the Holy Spirit from the wounds of Jesus. A constant recourse to her and a total imitation of her is necessary to this vocation and to any advancement in the prayer life.

When we consecrate ourselves to Mary we no longer belong to ourselves but to her, then our life and prayer become hers. Our intentions in prayer are no longer our own. The soul that belongs to her cannot even ask God anything ardently without feeling urged to seek the approval of its Mother. It could not ask what she does not want. It feels a certain check on all its interior desires and an inclination not to want anything but what she wants. One's aspirations become Mary's and all personal intentions become hers and hers become one's own. To make the special effort to pray with Mary and to ask for her interior sentiments and thoughts every time we kneel down to pray, is to make rapid advancement in prayer. Gradually we come to pray as though *we were Mary* living again on earth, even without our knowing exactly how this came about.

In the beginning, we may be aware of her presence on certain days especially dedicated to her or during certain seasons, such as great feasts or during the month of May which is dedicated to her. Or we may recognize Mary's action in certain graces and blessings granted us. That is to say, at first she is experienced more sensibly. Later on in the spiritual life, she is recognized more interiorly and spiritually and in conjunction with the action of the Holy Spirit within the soul. It is as though she passes into our souls and acts from within by the gift of her own interior action. She moves us from within, along with, and by the power of, the Holy Spirit Whose action comes into our souls because of her prayer. It is He Who puts Mary in our lives and into our interior dispositions, aspirations and sentiments; and it is Mary who draws Him into our souls. The Holy Spirit comes wherever He sees His mystic Spouse present. He acts more powerfully wherever she is allowed complete freedom in the soul.

It is Mary and the Holy Spirit Who transform us into Jesus. Then, when Jesus takes over the interior of our life she, as it were, hides behind Jesus and effaces her action to give place to Him. Or rather, her action is fused into His. Jesus and Mary, so to speak, place the soul between them and love each other through the soul so that it is transformed by the passage of their breath of love through it. We become Mary, loving, praising, adoring and caring for Jesus, and we are Jesus loving, praising, and caring for Mary. Prayer then, becomes easy, even in times of darkness and dryness, because we place ourselves in the double current of their constant prayer and allow Jesus and Mary to pray to the Father in the Spirit through and in the little temple of our souls.

To say our vocal prayers with and in Mary and Jesus is to learn to relish their sweetness as we could never do otherwise. The Litany of Loretto is a special joy when each title of Mary is offered to her as though we were her Son praising her with His lips and all the power of His word. When we call her Mirror of Justice, Seat of Wisdom, House of Gold, Ark of the Covenant, all the splendor of the mystic meaning is renewed in her soul and she overflows with joy to hear her Son confer on her anew the substantial glory that these titles convey. Jesus

Himself loves to give His Mother the honor of these praises again and again through our lips and to blot out all the evil words spoken against her. We can give Jesus and Mary the same joy in uttering the words of the Hail Mary to her in the Person of Jesus or to recite the Our Father in the person of Mary. One of the most efficacious and recollected means of singing the Divine Office is to say each Psalm in the Person of Jesus or Mary according as the content of the verses suggests.

No matter what the subject or content of our prayer, we will always be more recollected, more intimate, more confident, more enlightened, more loving, in the company of Mary. We will share her profound concentration on God in the Person of Jesus when we ask her to be with us in prayer. When we forget to invoke Mary, experience will prove to us that we are frequently distracted and for longer periods of time. But when we ask her grace, she keeps us attentive or recalls our minds to recollection much sooner than if they were left to themselves. We wander less in Mary's company and we do not wander so far away when she is by our side. With Mary we are more at ease in prayer because she teaches a reverent but loving familiarity with Jesus Who in turn brings us to the Father. With Mary our Mother we more easily find our rightful place in the family of God. We find Jesus in the crib, at Nazareth, on the Cross, or in the Eucharist more accessible, and we know just what to say to Him when our Mother is with us there.

When we are cold, distracted, dispirited and helpless, all we need to do is cry for our Mother and she will come with her spirit of love and light and prayer. Prayers which formerly were only words become full of meaning, and the specific tone of each, whether praise, sorrow, lament, desire, faith, or longing become more ardent, more intense, more pure and more specifically our own because we begin to see our own life experience in them. When we say our prayers with Mary we find them full of rich thought and insight, deep feeling and something of her own burning love, and if we allow her full scope in our souls they will become melted into that incandescent white heat of the purest love which is her own Immaculate Heart.

This does not mean that she will not sometimes, and even often, leave us in coldness, aridity and darkness. She is too much of a Mother not to allow us to taste all the bitterness of the Cross that will make us grow up in Christ. But even then, the dryness and affliction will bear the special mark of her presence and the sweet strength of peaceful contentment with whatever she provides for us. Because of her, bitterness becomes sweet even while it loses none of its bitterness, and this is a mystery of the Cross that only experience can prove. She stood at the Cross for us so that we could find the unction of love there with and in her. She stands beside us when we hang on our cross at prayer, to feed us secretly with the hidden manna of peaceful conformity in trial which she merited for us with and from Jesus. She teaches us to rejoice when we find no satisfaction in anything, if only we can give Him some, because that was the whole desire of her life: to love Him at her own expense. Thus we come to learn in each particular form of prayer, whether vocal or mental, whether in general recollection during work, or public liturgical acts, how to identify ourselves with Mary the Mystical Rose, and to experience that it is no longer I who now pray, but Mary who prays in me, and if Mary prays in me Jesus is being formed in me.

## XI. CONCLUSION

The life of the Christian is docility to the Holy Spirit. It is experiencing the Christ-life within us every day and letting Jesus live, love, suffer, sorrow, rejoice and pray in us when He wills and as He wills. Prayer gives us His mind. We become heavenly-minded people and then we begin to see things, events and other people through the eyes of Jesus. With Mary we will come to experience what St. Teresa taught us about prayer, especially that it is more important to know *Him to Whom we are praying*, than to know specific things to pray about. Prayer is a living conversation with the Divine Lover of our souls and once we have met Him personally we will want to surrender ourselves entirely to Him while He teaches us the lesson of His greatness and our nothingness. Then, when our experienced weakness compels us to perfect abandonment, all our activity will be directed and exercised by Him. Jesus will live in us, and that is the life of prayer.

Our final counsels then, must be that we should pray as we can, not as we cannot, according to St. Teresa:

> I only want you to be warned that, if you would progress a long way on this road and ascend to the Mansions of your desire, the impor-

tant thing is not to think much, but to love much; *do, then, whatever most arouses you to love. (Interior Castle*, IV, ch. 1:7)

This was her method of prayer. We must gently adapt ourselves to the way pointed out by her whom Pope Paul VI has called the Doctor of the Royal Road of Prayer (Address for the conferral of the Doctorate to St. Teresa of Jesus, Sept. 29, 1970). But we must pray in the manner that the Holy Spirit and Mary are directing us. We will only learn that lesson if we pray much. When prayer is hard, it is because we have not prayed enough. The more we do it the easier it will become. The person in love with God wants to spend all his or her time with Him and is alert to find any spare moment to speak with Him. We can always pray, we can always speak to God and listen to Him, in whatever state we find ourselves, so that there is no excuse for not praying or letting ourselves fall away from prayer. Everyone can pray, everyone has the ability to pray. And if a person is really sincere with God there is no such thing as bad prayer or praying the wrong way even if we are disappointed with our particular hours of prayer because they are difficult or lacking in consolation or success according to our way of thinking. Prayer is an effort of faith reaching out to God and its value or success comes from our disposition toward Him.

The degree and quality of our faith is the measure of our prayer. No state of prayer, even the most advanced, can be maintained without specific acts of faith, no matter how simple and few these may be. Even when the soul is wrapped in the silent embrace of the Blessed Trinity in the Seventh Mansions of the Castle, it will need to make specific interior acts of prayer from time to time. The soul ascends to God through these acts of knowledge and love, and one should follow the inclination of grace in making them.

The aim of our prayer is not to have thoughts about God, or to be always overflowing with affection, but to *possess God* and to *be moved by His Spirit* in all our actions. Real prayer will increasingly lift us above passing moods of depression, and disappointments will no longer weigh us down or influence our decisions. We will find ourselves more inclined to live every moment in a disposition of ready surrender to whatever comes rather than making particular resolutions for this or that. If we live in this trustful surrender, we will find that Christ Himself takes over our resolutions and acts in us without that studied effort for virtue which is always marked by at least some strain. Abiding in His love, virtue flows graciously and easily, and when falls come, they do not cast us down or surprise us. We can fall through sheer frailty and still remain in His love. This abiding in His love is the most apostolic activity in the world as St. John of the Cross tells us in the *Spiritual Canticle:*

> For a little of this pure love is more precious to God and the soul and more beneficial to the Church, even though it seems one is doing nothing, than all these other works put together. (st. 29:2)

The efficacy of the apostolic life of the Church is as *intense* and *rich as the interior life.* This interior life is the responsibility of every Christian. It is prayer which keeps the heat and light generating and the blood circulating through the whole body.

In conclusion, there are these little summary paragraphs on prayer from three great Carmelite saints which will serve to encapsulate the doctrine of prayer and fix it more deeply in our minds. The Lord is within us in the heaven of our souls, which thought was the great delight of St. Teresa and Sister Elizabeth of the Trinity. We can speak to Him as we would to our own Father in darkness or light as simply as St. Therese.

> Do you suppose it is of little importance that a soul which is often distracted should come to understand this truth and to find that, in order to speak to its Eternal Father and to take its delight in Him, it has no need to go to Heaven or to speak to Him in a loud voice? However quietly we speak, He is so near that He will hear us; we need no wings to go in search of Him but have only to find a place where we can be alone and look upon Him present within us. Nor need we feel strange in the presence of so kind a Guest; we must talk to Him very humbly, as we should to our father, ask Him for things as we should ask a father, tell Him our troubles, beg Him to put them right, and yet realize that we are not worthy to be called His children. (*Way of Perfection*, ch. 28:2)

> God in me and I in Him: let that be our motto. How wonderful is this presence of God in us, in the inner sanctuary of one's soul! There we always find Him, even though we no longer feel His presence; but He is there all the same, even

closer, as you said. That is where I love to look for Him. Let us try never to leave Him alone, so that our lives may be an unceasing prayer. (*Spiritual Writings*, Sister Elizabeth of the Trinity, p. 32)

*Let us lose ourselves in this Holy Trinity*, in this God Who is all Love. Let Him carry us off to those spheres where there is no one but Him, Him alone! There is a Being Who is Love and Who wants us to live in "fellowship" with Him. He is there within me, keeping me company, helping me to suffer, teaching me to go beyond my suffering to rest in Him. (Ibid., p. 33)

*I have found my heaven for Heaven is God and God is in my soul. (Reminiscences* of Sister Elizabeth of the Trinity)

How great is the power of prayer! One could call it a Queen who has at each instant free access to the King and who is able to obtain whatever she asks. To be heard it is not necessary to read from a book some beautiful formula composed for the occasion. If this were the case, alas, I would have to be pitied! Outside of the Divine Office which I am very unworthy to recite, I do not have the courage to force myself to search out beautiful prayers in books. There are so many of them it really gives me a headache! And each prayer is more beautiful than the others. I cannot recite them all and not knowing which to choose, I do like children who do not know how to read, I say very simply to God what I wish to say, without composing beautiful sentences, and He always understands me. For me, prayer is an aspiration of the heart, it is a simple glance directed to heaven, it is a cry of gratitude and love in the midst of trial as well as joy; finally, it is something great, supernatural, which expands my soul and unites me to Jesus.

... Sometimes when my mind is in such a great aridity that it is impossible to draw forth one single thought to unite me with God, I very slowly recite an "Our Father," and then the angelic salutation; then these prayers give me great delight; they nourish my soul much more than if I had recited them precipitately a hundred times. (*Story of a Soul*, trs. John Clarke, O.C.D., ICS publications, Institute of Carmelite Studies; Washington, D.C., 1975)

# XII. PERSONAL NOTES AND COMMENTS

# PERSONAL NOTES AND COMMENTS

# PERSONAL NOTES AND COMMENTS

# PERSONAL NOTES AND COMMENTS